Also by Derek Tangye

TIME WAS MINE

ONE KING

WENT THE DAY WELL (Editor)

A GULL ON THE ROOF

A CAT IN THE WINDOW

A DRAKE AT THE DOOR

A DONKEY IN THE MEADOW

LAMA

THE WAY TO MINACK

A CORNISH SUMMER

COTTAGE ON A CLIFF

A CAT AFFAIR

Derek Tangye

SUN ON THE LINTEL

ILLUSTRATED BY JEAN TANGYE

London
MICHAEL JOSEPH

First published in Great Britain by Michael Joseph Ltd
52 Bedford Square, London WC1B 3EF
1976

© 1976 by Derek Tangye

ISBN 0 7181 1536 8

Set and printed in Great Britain by
Ebenezer Baylis and Son Ltd,
The Trinity Press, Worcester, and London

To Anthea

ONE

New Year's Day and a black easterly was blowing in from the sea and The Lizard.

'I want you to listen to me.'

'I'm listening.'

From where I was standing with my back to the fireplace, my head level with the great granite lintel which had been heaved into place when the cottage was built five hundred years before, I could see Jeannie in our galley of a kitchen, concentrating on a recipe book open before her.

'You're not listening,' I said, 'or if you're listening, you're not hearing.'

'I won't be a second.'

A problem of two people being happy together is that they talk too much to each other. A thought comes into the head, and it has to be shared. They are inclined to prattle, gushing their thoughts into words, hoping for instant reaction from the other.

'It's not important,' I said, 'it can wait.'

The kitchen is very small, eight feet long and five across; and yet it has numerous small cupboards with natural wood doors that go from floor to ceiling, an electric stove, a sink, a dishwasher, a refrigerator, a Kenwood Chef, and of course a space where the food is

7

prepared. Jeannie drew the design for the kitchen, though it was I who, from time to time, had insisted on buying the electrical extras.

But at first I was against the installation of electricity. For ten years Jeannie and I had lived with paraffin and calor gas and an old petrol pump which had brought the water up from our well; and we were content. There were no groans from Jeannie when she cooked breakfast on the paraffin stove, no groans from me when I dipped the lighter into the methylated spirit bottle, then fixed it to the paraffin lamp, lit it, waited for its warmth to light the mantle of the lamp, then pumped it into brightness. There was pleasure in these basic acts. A sense of freedom in being so dependent on primitive necessities.

It was during this period that we learnt to distrust a world in which the people threw up their hands in horror if there were a bread delivery strike, an electricity strike, a milkman's strike, or any strike which interrupted the conveyor belt method of their living. It seemed to us that the people had created a spiritual vacuum, so that they possessed no peace of mind once a cog in their material existence jammed.

We had our problems, many of them, but we appreciated that the base of happiness did not depend upon man-made technical tricks. We could survive happily without electricity, or main water, or a telephone. These, we learnt, were not the essentials for a happy life. We were spared, also, from any 'keep up with the Joneses' attitude because we had no Joneses to keep up with. We never had to suffer from that material hunger which has no end to its appetite. True, occasionally we would have happy times with witty friends, lots of laughter, jokes at other people's expense, a wish superficially to please . . . but we were aware, as we poured out the drinks and laughed and listened and enjoyed such moments of gaiety, that we were living again our London selves which we had run away from. For I had learnt that gregariousness hides you from yourself, and that if you want to know the real truth of living it is found in solitude. Then, if you are patient, a window opens upon a multitude of subtleties to which you were blind and deaf before. You even become aware of man's trivial living time, and marvel at the conceit with which he fills it.

Then one day the electricity planners came to Minack, part of a scheme to steer this part of the Land's End peninsula into the modern era; and I proceeded to object to the wooden poles which were to come through our wood, refused to have one planted adjacent to the cottage, later insisted that one pole should have a couple of feet cut off because it appeared above the tops of the trees. I was like a tribesman in the jungle, whose instinct was against the benefit of change.

I did not, however, obstinately maintain this attitude once the electricity was installed. True, I continued to resent the fact that, instead of sitting in a cottage which was totally independent of the outside world, I was now tied by a cable to a generating station . . . but, at the same time, I began to learn to accept the advantages. I learnt, for instance, that the simple life can be enhanced by modern gadgets; and once converted to this point of view, I behaved as a convert is inclined to do. My enthusiasm for the cause became greater than that of those who were born to it.

Jeannie, for instance, was suspicious of dish-washers until I arrived home with one in the back of the car after I had been to St Ives to pay a visit to the dentist. A shop next door had a dishwasher displayed in the window, and when I came out of the dentist's, bemused perhaps by what had been done to me, I went into the shop and bought it. It was a whim, a sudden act which had to be done before I thought twice about it, even before I knew how it could be squeezed into the kitchen; and to make sure there would not be a moment's delay before its installation, I called on a plumber friend, and he came out to Minack that same day. It is so important never to delay turning a whim into reality.

There was also sense in my extravagance. Electricity now provided the opportunity of saving Jeannie tedious work, and so gave her the opportunity to make use of her talents. Jeannie finds, like many of us, that manual labour is easier than mental labour. Hence, instead of writing or painting, she will gladly undertake any task such as ironing, making an unnecessary cake, weeding the garden, rather than concentrate her mind on the tasks her talents deserve of her. It was because of this attitude of hers that I once regularly kept her locked in the wood cabin where we bunched violets in our early days at Minack, a cabin which has since been joined to the cottage and become a spare bedroom, in order to make certain that she completed her book *Meet me at the Savoy*; and I repeated the exercise when she wrote her novel *Hotel Regina*, and again when she wrote *Home is the Hotel*. I too, however, am a dallyer, and so I do not complain if she, in turn, locks my door when I am working.

'I'm ready,' said Jeannie, closing the recipe book, 'what is it you want to say?'

'I want to list my New Year resolutions.'

She laughed. 'How very funny.'

'I'm serious.'

'Oh really. . . .'

New Year resolutions are, of course, a perennial joke. They are made to be broken. As a twelve-year-old I resolved to read a page of a French book every day of the holidays . . . this resolution lasted two days.

'There are certain things I want to do,' I said, 'and I am always putting off doing them. Sensible things. And perhaps if I parcel them together in a package of New Year resolutions I might make myself carry them out.'

'Perhaps. . . .'

Jeannie, however, is less of a dallyer than I am. I am naturally lazy. I gaze into space, I meander on a walk, I roam around mental corners before making a decision . . . unless an incident suddenly inspires my imagination. Then I act quickly.

Jeannie is inclined always to act quickly. She is like a rider who fearlessly jumps fences, not worrying what may happen on the other side. When we were making up our minds whether to leave London and make a new life at Minack, it was Jeannie who led me to the decision. I wavered. I foresaw the problems. But Jeannie, once her mind was made up, had no doubts; and when she closed the door of suite 205, her office at the Savoy Hotel, for the last time, she had no fear of the future. She, who was the personal friend of the great names of an era, showed no hesitation in exchanging her luxury life for a Cornish cottage which had no running water, or bathroom, or electricity. She had decided where the true values lay, and in the years we have been at Minack I have never known her question the correctness of her judgement. Not even in some emotional moment has she declared her wish to return. Not even when she has received handsome offers to do so, like the time she was asked to handle the publicity for Charlie Chaplin's last movie. Minack was her harbour, and that was all there was to it.

'All right,' she said, curling herself on the sofa, 'tell me about your resolutions.'

Jeannie is slim and dark, and a mixture of Scots, Irish and English. Sometimes I have clear evidence of the Scot in her, sometimes of the Irish, sometimes of the English. This means that my life with her has never been dull.

'Well,' I said, pausing for a moment while I prised out with a matchstick the ash remnants of my pipe into the ashtray on my desk, 'I want to start my New Year resolutions with what I am doing now . . . instead of spilling the ash carelessly on the desk, which it is my habit to do, I'm going to knock the ash cleanly into the ashtray like so. . . .'

The ash, with the aid of the matchstick and a knock, fell neatly into the tray.

'That's a good start,' said Jeannie laughing, 'what next?'

The surge of enthusiasm one has about New Year resolutions is intoxicating. A glorious self-confidence overwhelms one.

'I'm not going to be bossed by Oliver and Ambrose,' I said, 'nor by Penny and Fred.'

'I think you're rather hard on them!'

'Not at all,' I said firmly, 'I think there's something weak about my character the way I pander to them. I'm going to correct this.'

'How so?'

I realised there was a hint of defiance in my voice, a tone of aggressiveness which one adopts when intending to change course from the accepted routine.

'For instance,' I said, 'Oliver and Ambrose are infiltrating more and more into our lives. Before long you'll find they'll stop sleeping in the porch and be on our bed instead.'

'What would be wrong in that?'

'What would be wrong? My dear girl, I have spent most of my married life with a cat on the bed, first Monty then Lama, and the prospect of having two on the bed is impossible to contemplate.'

'We'll see.'

'You won't get round me this time. None of you will.'

Of course, she knew that my attitude was a vulnerable one. When I first met Monty, the beautiful ginger cat who came with us to Minack when we left London, he was playing with a string on the green carpet of Jeannie's office at the Savoy. He was a tiny kitten, obtained by Jeannie's mother from a hairdresser's in St Albans, and I, a cat hater, was expected to be thrilled by the sight of him. 'I'll throw him over Hammersmith Bridge on the way home,' I murmured threateningly. But Monty passed safely over the bridge, and on into Barnes and to Mortlake, where he lived for the next seven years in our cottage on the river overlooking the finishing post of the Boat Race, then to another seven happy years at Minack. He conquered me, enslaved me, and when he died I swore I would never have another cat.

I did, however, in this moment of sad emotion, add a curious condition. Curious, because at the time I was not hoping that it would come true. I said to Jeannie that the only way in which I would ever have another cat was if it were all black, came to us in a storm and there was no trace whence it came. Lama fulfilled these conditions. Lama, who sat on my lap for hour after hour while I wrote my books about Minack, was all black, came to us in a storm, and came from no human home we could trace. Like Monty, she became the repository of my secret thoughts. As with Monty, I began to be afraid when she grew old.

Three years before she died, however, another black cat started to appear regularly in the vicinity of Minack, and we had reason to believe that it was the same black kitten we once discovered in a small cave down the cliff. The mother of the kitten was a little wild grey cat, whom we always considered to be Lama's mother, and in that case the kitten and Lama were relations. The kitten had certainly looked exactly like Lama when she was young . . . and the black cat which now had appeared had the same uncanny resemblance. The same shaped head, the same compact body, and only the tail was different. Lama had a plushy tail, that of the new arrival was thin like a twig.

I told what happened during these three years in *A Cat Affair*. Oliver, as we called the black cat, persistently stayed in the neighbourhood, though at first he was far too nervous for us ever to approach him. It seemed that, though he wanted to be near us, he did not yet expect to be part of us; and this, of course, was fortunate because our love centred around Lama, and on no account did we want her peaceful routine disturbed. But, as time went by, Oliver slowly became more confident. We had now to be on guard that there was no confrontation; and, although come near enough to be touched. If either of us stooped to stroke him as he drank his milk, he would dash away. He had no wish to be seduced by human condescension. He intended to keep his independence. He didn't want to fall a victim to flattery.

And then he began to falter. Though still elusive, he began to show an interest in comfort. The successful rebel, who reluctantly becomes aware of some of the advantages of the establishment. I saw the danger signals. I realised he could be skilful enough to worm his way into the establishment and, in a little while, boss it.

'I absolutely refuse,' I therefore repeated to Jeannie, 'ever to have those two cats sleeping on our bed. One resolution I certainly mean to keep.'

'Bravo,' Jeannie replied in an off-hand way, stroking Oliver who, a second before, had jumped on her lap.

The donkeys, Penny and her son Fred, had a less obvious way of interfering with the pattern of my life. They interfered by staring at me. They stared whenever they wanted to be moved from one meadow to another, or when they decided they would like a walk along the cliff path towards Lamorna, or when they were bored and wanted to be amused. I would come out of the cottage in the morning, intent on pursuing some personal task, then observe that the donkeys were staring at me and, if I took no notice of them, hooting at me. They had a subtle form of blackmail . . . if you love us, as you say you do, prove it.

Of course, it was always pleasant to prove it. I had been proving it constantly from the first time I saw Penny, an emaciated black donkey standing in a field outside the Plume of Feathers at Scorrier, a field which has now become the concrete beginning of the Redruth by-pass . . . from the moment I first saw Fred, born to Penny a month later. I was always yielding to them both, especially in the mornings when I had letters to write, bills to pay, accounts to unravel, for then they gave me a chance to change my plans. 'Oh well,' I would say to Jeannie, 'it's a lovely day, let's take them for a walk.' I would thereupon revel in the hour and a half that followed, though when I returned, when I arrived back at the cottage to pursue the tedious duties I had set myself, I would find that my good intentions had disappeared. The letters, the bills, the accounts, would remain untouched.

I can, perhaps, plead justification for this dilatory behaviour because of the kind of life we led at Minack. We felt detached from the outside world. The outside world, it seemed, was imposed upon by publicity-minded men and women who, in order to maintain the momentum of their ambitions, thrust their views upon the public, irrespective of whether these views mirrored sincerity. Thus, ugly moods and situations which might have faded into oblivion, were magnified into major issues; and grievances, real or imaginary, were manoeuvred on to national platforms; and, at all times, envy was worshipped. Yet the pressure of modern life is such that the people accept the brainwashers. They have no time or energy to challenge them. Materialism is all that matters; and survival.

We, too, have our materialistic problems. We, too, are influenced by the brainwashers. We, too, have tensions. But we are among the lucky ones because our environment gives us the chance to see our lives in perspective; and if we do not take this chance to do so it is our fault alone. We are not rushed. We wake up to the sound of gulls crying, instead of traffic. We have no office to hasten to, no clocking in at a factory, no days ahead full of strain-filled appointments. Thus time is inclined to stand still, and we dream, and we stare out across the moorland to the blue expanse of Mount's Bay, and engross ourselves in small, unimportant pleasures; and then feel guilty over such periods of pleasant idleness. The donkeys made me feel guilty.

'Nor am I going to be bossed by the donkeys,' I said to Jeannie. 'No more walks in the morning when I have other things to do. No more being hypnotised by their stare.'

'He's tough,' said Jeannie, stroking Oliver between his ears. 'You and the donkeys will have to look out this year.'

'It's for my own protection.'

'Why?'

'I want to be organised. I want to be like one of those people who have their desks neat, their lives orderly, who are able to do all sorts of things which I never have the time for.'

'And you blame Oliver, Ambrose, Penny and Fred for your present failure?'

She was teasing me.

'Yes,' I said, playing up to her.

I walked over to the wicker basket beside the fire, picked up a log, and placed it in the grate.

'What else,' she went on with mock solemnity, 'have you in mind for your list of resolutions?'

'I'm going to grow our own plants for the garden,' I said, 'and I'll write out a list of the seeds we want during the course of this week. I'm not going to bother Percy this year.'

Percy Potter was in charge of the Sutton Seed Trial Grounds at Gulval outside Penzance, a master gardener, who provides a superb display of summer colour in the gardens overlooking Mount's Bay, and who, in other years, had often provided us with plants.

'That's a good idea. More?'

'Make up our minds whether we can continue with the flower farm, wages and costs being what they are.'

'That's a serious resolution. I don't want to hear about that.'

'It will have to be faced.'

'Perhaps . . . but I only want to hear about the fun resolutions.'

'Well,' I said, 'I intend to become a cook.'

17

'Wonderful!'

'Don't forget I used to cook. I gave you your first lesson.'

'Hardly.'

'Well, that first meal you cooked for me . . . the bubble and squeak, I mean. You didn't even know you had to put fat in the frying pan first.'

'I have progressed since then!'

'You certainly have . . . and now I would like to compete with you.'

'It will be a relief for me if you do. What sort of cooking have you in mind?'

'Do you remember that Prunier dish I did one day in Mortlake just before we came to Minack'

'Years ago, and I will never forget it.'

'Prawns and lemon sole and rice, and the hours I took over the sauce?'

'Sheer artistry.'

'That's the kind of cooking I would like to do again.'

'A great occasion it will be, if it comes off.'

Oliver, at that moment purring on her lap, pressed his claws into her leg. Ecstacy on his part, pain on hers.

'Oliver . . . don't!'

And Oliver jumped to the floor.

'Any more resolutions?'

'Oh yes,' I said, 'plenty . . . but I think I'll keep them to myself. It will be safer.'

'I won't broadcast them.'

'One of them I'll tell you about,' I said, 'is my intention to read *Remembrance of Things Past* again.'

'I never reached further than *Swann's Way*.'

'Well, I never read all of it. I skipped a lot. But that doesn't alter the fact that Proust had a huge influence on me when I was young. At the time I believed my personal thoughts, my personal fears and contradictions were exclusively my own. Proust showed me they were not.'

'He helped to guide your growing up.'

'Yes. I would like to find out what effect he would have on me now.'

A gull was crying on the roof. Probably Philip. He was an old gull and he made a habit of coming when the other two regulars, Flotsam and Jetsam, were absent. He had special treatment when he was on his own, a slice of meat or of cake.

'I also,' I said, 'intend to go through the papers stacked in Labour Warms.'

Jeannie was laughing.

'There are oceans of letters and notes and papers!'

'That's what I mean. It's time we sorted them out.'

Labour Warms was an institution in my life. A massive teak cupboard that was in my nursery at 48 Bramham Gardens, Kensington, then in my nursery at Glendorgal, our one-time family home near Newquay in Cornwall. Then it was installed in my bachelor flat in Elm Park Garden Mews near the Kings Road, and later followed me to Cholmondley House on the river at Richmond, and after that to Thames Bank Cottage at Mortlake. It was a family heirloom, a reminder of Victorian solidity, of the British Empire at its peak . . . and across the top of the cupboard, painted in blue against the brown of the teak, was the warning:

LABOUR WARMS. SLOTH HARMS.

An appropriate motto, it seemed, for the coming year.

TWO

I have seldom been the person I wished to be, because the person I wished to be changed so quickly that I was unable to catch him. My Walter Mittys have been numerous.

Sometimes I have wished to be a steady, conventional type, playing safe. Sometimes I have wished to live a Bohemian life as varied as that of Augustus John. Sometimes I have wished to be a pianist, sometimes an England cricketer, sometimes an art collector. Sometimes I have wished to enjoy the deceptive applause of transient success, sometimes to run away from it and hide. Sometimes I have wished to be an intellectual, praised by the few, though unintelligible to the many. Sometimes I have wished to be gregarious among the sophisticated, sometimes to live the life of a hermit. Walter Mittys have filtered through my life, changing their roles with bewildering rapidity, providing me in their aftermath with many conclusions. Among them is a distaste for those who relish exercising power over their fellow human beings; another is that a fundamental contemporary need is to delve into one's own secret thoughts before becoming anaesthetised by the opinions of a crowd . . . and another is my everlasting gratitude to the Walter Mitty who led me to Minack.

On New Year's Day, however, it was a Walter Mitty

of good intentions who had embraced me . . . but who, within twenty-four hours, had deserted me.

I had sat down in the corner of the sofa for a moment, when Oliver jumped on my lap . . . just after breakfast, and I was about to go to my desk and answer letters.

'Oliver,' I said, 'get off. I don't want anything to do with you!'

Purr, purr.

'Oliver,' I repeated, though I cursed the half-hearted tone which had crept into my voice, 'get off. I have other things to do.'

Purr, purr.

It was as if I had Lama on my lap again. The same silky black fur, the same neat head, the same unwillingness on my part to move.

'Jeannie,' I called out, 'please help me!'

The same cry as many times before. The same wish for a diversion. A saucer of milk or of fish. Anything to lure away the purr on my lap.

'You're too indecisive,' she said, coming in from the porch and proceeding to fulfil the task expected of her. 'All you have to do is to push him off.'

Quite so. All I had to do was to push him off, and yet a part of me refused to act. Why?

I had a special reason. I remembered the three years before Lama died when I had treated Oliver as a pariah, shouting him away from the cottage, frightening him by savagely scraping my feet on the gravel if he advanced too close. I had aimed to make him feel unwanted, hoping to force him back to the place whence he came, and so leave Lama in peace. I didn't care how unhappy I made him provided Lama continued her reign undisturbed. Lama belonged to Minack. Oliver was an interloper.

Propinquity, however, is a danger. A relationship between two people can blossom when their work brings them together, or they share a regular journey, or other circumstances beyond their control make them see each other often. Against their will they begin to love. Against my will, Oliver began to creep into my affection.

It was his persistence that caused this. He was so determined to become a part of Minack that he was prepared to accept any insults and much discomfort. When he first began to hover around the neighbourhood, and for many months afterwards, he used to sleep at night on a bank of grass and bracken beside the lane on the far side of Monty's Leap. He huddled himself into a little cavity, seemingly unperturbed by the rain and the gales; and in the daytime he would sit for hours by the white gate staring up towards the cottage, fleeing away into the undergrowth whenever we walked towards him. Minack was a magnet, but it gave him no confidence.

Jeannie, in her role as a lifetime lover of all cats, was the first to show pity; and she found a wooden box which she placed in the undergrowth near the white gate, lining it with straw. Oliver liked it immediately; and later I improved this dwelling by covering it with polythene and hiding it with bracken, and making a tunnel of an entrance, and a back exit out of which he could escape if frightened by an inquisitive fox. Our mistake, however, was the choice of site. It was close to a gully, and when the gully was flooded by the winter rains so too was Oliver's dwelling. The morning following the first flood, I found him perched on the branch of an old gorse bush, miaowing. I thereupon rebuilt his dwelling elsewhere.

Some time after this episode, I saw him hobbling up the lane towards the cottage on three legs. Lama was out of the cottage at the time and, at first, I thought it was she who had been injured. From a distance they looked so exactly alike that it was easy to make such an error, and I called out to Jeannie: 'Lama's coming up the lane and there's something wrong with one of her legs!' Jeannie, who was in the tiny front garden, called back that I had made the usual mistake: 'It's Oliver, not Lama . . . Lama is with me!'

I watched Oliver hobble up the lane, then turn right into the stone building which serves as the garage and disappear under the Volvo. I had never seen him behave in such a determined fashion, nor had I ever seen him go into the garage before. His back legs were sound, so also the right front one, but I clearly saw the left one was dangling.

'Oliver needs your help, Jeannie . . . you'll have to examine him.'

'But he would never let me!'

'You'll have to try.'

To her surprise, Oliver this time showed no fear of her. He remained quite still as she examined him and found that his paw had a deep cut.

'Looks as if he's been caught in a snare.'

'Damn them,' I said.

Each day he let her bathe it with the liquid of Exultation of Flowers that comes from Nairn in Scotland, and a bottle of which Jeannie always keeps handy . . . and, after a week, the wound was healed. But, by that time, our relationship with Oliver had changed. He had won a victory, and he knew it. From now on Jeannie and I were on the retreat, facing the fact that he was here to stay. The prospect did not please us. For Lama's sake, we now had to be prepared to chase away a cat who had won our affection.

There are, of course, many who would call our attitude a sentimental absurdity. Why bother about the feelings of a cat? Why waste time on animal love when the human race can obliterate itself at the touch of a button; when twisted minds leave random bombs in crowded places; when schoolchildren threaten their teachers with flick knives; when there is a perpetual economic crisis? Animal love, in such circumstances, does seem absurd. It is an irrelevancy compared with the problems of the day. No wonder that pragmatic people condemn animal lovers. Life is too serious for such indulgence.

Unashamedly, however, Jeannie and I allow ourselves

such indulgence. Animals offer stability in this unstable world. They do not deceive. They soothe jittery moods. They offer solace in times of trouble by the way they listen to you. They may not understand a word you say, but that doesn't matter, because it is a dumb sympathy that you ask of them and they give it; an extra-sensory understanding, which is the more comforting since it is secret. You have no regrets afterwards for having disclosed too much.

I am not, on the other hand, an indiscriminate animal lover. Indiscriminate animal lovers can be so lavish in their love that they seem to suffer from a form of disease. Their emotions are highly pitched, and they agonise over the welfare of animals to such an extent that their home lives become warped . . . horses, ponies, donkeys, lost dogs, cats and kittens, and any other unhappy animal they may find, take over. I admire the selflessness of such people, but I have to admit my love for animals does not embrace such selflessness. My love for an animal is based on a friendship, and I cannot offer this to animals in quantity. I want it to be concentrated on the few. If I once allowed myself to succumb to the lost look of the animal kingdom, I too would catch the disease. I would lose my sense of proportion.

Sometimes, however, I have been close to catching the disease. I am, for instance, irrational as far as snares and the trapping of animals are concerned. When we first came to Minack, gin traps were still legal, and we used to listen to the trapper hammering into the ground the stake to which the trap was attached, knowing that in the evening the cries of the trapped rabbits would begin. First a number of cries after the rabbits had come out from their burrows, then more spasmodically during the course of the night. It was a brutal experience and, when the day came when Monty was caught in one of the traps, our emotions exploded. Jeannie picked up the trap after we had released him and flung it away into the undergrowth . . .

24

only to receive a visit from an angry farmer, who accused both ourselves and Monty of trespassing. He was justified in doing so, and I had no right to argue. We were newly arrived city folk, who did not understand the standards of those who had long experience of the land. Rabbits to us were pretty things, but to the farmer they were vermin . . . like mice in the kitchen.

When the gin trap became illegal, the rabbits had already been obliterated by myxomatosis and, for some years, there was peace at night in the countryside. Then the rabbits gradually returned and large scale snaring began, and the snares are more diabolical in many ways than gin traps. A snare, for instance, can catch an animal around its body and squeeze it; and, apart from rabbits, I have known many a cat caught in this manner. I haven't, however, seen a rabbit snare in this area for a long time because myxomatosis came back yet again and so there was no need for snares. Snares and gin traps, therefore, had become a part of unpleasant history, or so I thought. I had no idea that another kind of snare existed.

For a number of years, a group of influential Cornish farmers had been conducting a campaign alleging that badgers, the most hygienic in their habits of all British wild animals, were carriers of tuberculosis, and that they were the cause of tuberculosis in cattle. Cattle T.B. is obviously a serious matter and the Ministry of Agriculture takes every possible step to control it. The herd of each farm is regularly tested, and whenever an animal is found to be infected it is slaughtered. If a herd, therefore, is badly infected the financial loss to the farmer is severe.

The veterinary advisers of the Ministry of Agriculture have constantly been trying to discover the cause of the disease. One theory is that farmers overstock their land with cattle, producing conditions similar to those that account for T.B. in humans who live in overcrowded and underfed areas. Another theory is that the modern intensive method of farming and the use of chemical fertilisers are the cause. Theories have abounded, but without any fundamental evidence to support any one of them.

Thus some farmers became angry, mystified and frustrated, and began a witch-hunt against the badger; and they pressed the Ministry of Agriculture so successfully that the Ministry agreed to examine the health of badgers in the West Cornwall area. Badger dropping samples were to be sent for laboratory tests and bodies of dead badgers were to be examined. All this was a conscientious attempt to solve the T.B. problem and it had the advantage that, if the laboratory tests were to prove negative, badgers would be cleared conclusively as the cause of the trouble. The Ministry, however, did not disclose how the dead badgers were to be obtained. Jeannie and I were to find out.

Meanwhile, we have had our own badger problems. A badger, for instance, will sometimes take a fancy to a meadow of bulbs and proceed to dig up a patch, or he will roll on the daffodil foliage, or play a game in a meadow where the daffodils are soon to be picked. He will also keep obstinately to the track which his forbears have used for hundreds of years, and so, if the track runs across a daffodil meadow, nothing we can do will ever make him abandon it. These antics do not disturb us. No major harm occurs. We accept the badger presence.

I was not, however, so tolerant of the badger who developed a passion for carrots last summer. The carrots were sown in long double rows at monthly intervals in an area of ground beyond the greenhouses where we had our tomatoes. Nearby were rows of peas, runner beans, raspberry canes, lettuce, strawberries, turnips, beetroot and other produce of a kitchen garden for our own use . . . but the carrots, though we needed some for ourselves, were chiefly grown for the benefit of Penny and Fred. This was their winter fodder, succulent carrots which we would dry and store and produce by the handful for donkey delight when the grass in the fields had lost its nourishment. The first sowing was patiently weeded and thinned and, at last, had reached the stage ready for pulling, when overnight they disappeared. Fragments of carrot foliage lay scattered on the ground, but not a carrot was to be seen. It was as if foraging pigs had been let loose on the patch.

'Disaster!' I said to Geoffrey, our help, standing beside me. 'What are we going to do?'

'Can't do anything,' he replied, cheerfully. 'They've gone.'

'Of course they've gone,' I said, impatiently. Geoffrey is inclined to show a macabre jollity when things go wrong. 'But what are we going to do about it?'

'Dunno.'

I had heard in the past of badgers eating carrots, but they had never before come to Minack. We have had carrot-eating mice, and carrot-eating rabbits, but they had been leisurely eaters. They enjoyed their nibbles, then returned to their quarters. They never gorged a double row of carrots, each row seventy feet long, all in a night.

'Well,' I said, 'we have to save the next batch, and I've got an idea how to do it . . . we'll lay a roll of wire netting all along the two rows, flat on the foliage. A badger would never dare to go under that. He'll think it's a trap.'

'If he has a mind to do it, it won't work.'

'We'll try.'

The roll of wire netting was laid down, the slim young carrots began to bulge, and not one of them was disturbed.

'The trick is successful,' I said.

'Too soon to say that,' replied Geoffrey. 'The carrots aren't ready for pulling yet.'

And he was right. The day that the carrots were ready for pulling, the day that we were prepared to do so, a sequence of visitors arrived and the time was spent talking instead of pulling.

Next morning the carrot ground resembled the aftermath of a battlefield.

27

We still had a third batch of sowings and, this time, I said to Geoffrey it was up to him to devise their protection.

'I reckon,' he said, 'that he comes up from the cliff. I'll put wire netting along the cliff side and that will stop him.'

'What about the wood? He might come from there.'

'I don't reckon he will.'

So the cliff side of the greenhouse field was closed by wire netting, and the carrots were considered to be safe. As August arrived, they bulged in weight, and on a Friday night when I paid Geoffrey we agreed to pull them on Monday after he had picked the tomatoes.

On Sunday night, a moonlight night, I slept uneasily for reasons quite unconnected with carrots . . . and when, in the early hours of Monday morning, I was lying awake, my mind buzzing around without purpose, I thought to myself that I would be better off if I took a stroll. I might even have a look at the carrots.

I strolled down the lane, across Monty's Leap, and turned left through the gap. I walked quietly towards the wire gate Geoffrey had made, and into the kitchen garden . . . and within sight of the carrots. The moon was full, glinting on the glass of the greenhouses, shining on two annihilated rows of plump carrots . . . and on a badger. He was young, I could see that, and he was moving slowly and swaying. A badger bursting with carrots, and the pleasure of a wild night out. A badger without a care in the world; a glorious, self-indulgent sleep ahead of him, his mind awhirl, his belly full. He did not even notice me as I stepped up close to him. He had created, by his discovery of the donkey carrots, his perfect world. He was carrot-drunk.

How had he penetrated Geoffrey's wire netting? Simple. He had dug under it.

The incident caused me to contemplate how I would have felt if I had been a farmer with a field of carrots which had been destroyed by an army of badgers. My loss was comparatively small, although Penny and Fred would not consider it small. They had lost their winter fodder, but at least I could find something to replace it. A farmer, on the other hand, who has lost a crop also loses his income. It explains, perhaps, why some farmers are so ruthless in their attitude towards animal life. Survival is at stake, and a wild animal which threatens their livelihood is an enemy. Badgers, for instance, were enemies in the minds of those who believed they were the carriers of T.B. Any step to kill them was a good step.

One evening I saw two dogs hunting together on the other side of the valley towards Lamorna. They were tearing up and down a field, and dashing into the moorland and back again as if they were following a trail. I did not take much interest in them, except to be irritated by their barking, and I didn't notice their breed or recognise them as belonging to anyone I knew. They were obviously enjoying themselves and they could continue to do so as far as I was concerned. I reckoned they would not stay long in the neighbourhood, and the barking would cease and it would be quiet again.

An hour later, however, there was still the sound of barking; a muffled sound of barking, and I remarked to Jeannie that one of the dogs was likely to be at the entrance of a badger sett. This had happened before in the area concerned. A terrier of a Lamorna friend of mine used to scare his owner by going down into a badger sett, going so far that the barks became hardly audible. On this occasion, therefore, I continued to take little notice, and we had our supper of poached lemon sole, which came from the fish market at Newlyn, and listened afterwards to a Fauré concert from the Royal Festival Hall, and then went to bed early.

Our bedroom window faces across the shallow valley to the other side where I first saw the two dogs chasing the trail. We were lying there, hoping to sleep, and being checked from doing so by: 'Bark, bark!' It was a resigned bark. No urgency in it.

'The dog's getting tired,' I murmured to Jeannie. 'Will stop soon.'

'You don't think it's in trouble?'

'Of course not. It is an obstinate dog, which is frustrated. It's reached the end of the trail it followed, and now is baulked from fulfilment. It will tire before long, and go home.'

'Sure?'

'Yes . . . now go to sleep.'

I have always been vexed by three o'clock in the morning. Why is it that you can go relaxed to bed at ten, then wake up at three in a state of apprehension? All the mixed-up stresses are present. A challenge is too big to cope with. Your money affairs are insoluble. Your job in danger. You lie awake with your mind tight, ideas racing each other, and wonder how it is possible to survive. On this occasion, however, it was not personal apprehension that woke me up at three o'clock in the morning. The apprehension concerned the dog. I lay there in bed hearing it bark for half a minute, then silence for three, then another bark. Jeannie, too, had woken up.

'It *is* in trouble,' she said.

'Can't think how.'

A bark, silence, a bark.

'We had better get up and have a look.'

'Not yet,' I said. I was comfortable. I selfishly had no wish to leave the warmth of my bed to go searching for a dog in the dark. Anyhow, I said to myself, it couldn't be in serious trouble. There was nothing to cause a dog trouble. It wasn't as if the gin traps were still around. It was probably just waiting for a badger to come out of its sett, or a fox from its earth.

A long silence.

'There you are,' I said, sleepily. 'It's given up and gone home.'

Bark.

'You're wrong . . . come on, get up.'

30

I obeyed. I dressed, found the torch, a beam torch which shines like a searchlight, and we were about to set off when Jeannie said: 'You had better bring the secateurs.' I picked up a pair which were on the shelf in the porch and put them in my pocket. 'It may be lying hurt in a thicket,' she added, 'and we might have to cut our way through.'

We walked down the lane towards Monty's Leap, past the stables on our right, past two large shadows that loomed beside the hedge of the stable meadow. A soft whinnying noise sounded from one of the shadows.

'Quiet, Fred,' I said. 'We don't want any ballyhoo from you.'

Fred, if he saw us out at unusual hours, was inclined to announce the matter to the neighbourhood. I have known him shatter a soft summer night, soundless except for the sea lapping rocks, with a crescendo of blaring hee-haws.

'Quiet, Fred,' I repeated. And he was quiet.

We passed, and went on up the lane. It was a dark, moonless night and, therefore, we relied on the dog continuing to bark to give us our bearings. We trudged up a grass-covered path into the moorland, and then along a track bordered by blackberry brambles, and all the while the dog was silent. I was sure we were going in the right direction, but I knew that, unless the dog barked, we would never be able to find him. We had begun to walk downhill towards the sea when, suddenly, to my left I heard a kind of strangled cry of a dog, a sad cry, no bark this time. It was as if he had heard us and feared we would go by, and all his previous barking would be wasted. Yachtsmen in need of rescue must feel like that, when they watch a ship pass by without observing them.

'In there,' I said to Jeannie. 'Through that bracken, by that elder tree beside the hedge.' I was beaming the torch in that direction. 'That's where it is.'

We plunged into the high bracken, and I promptly fell over because I went too fast and a foot stepped into a hole. Then Jeannie did the same, and there we were, the two of

31

us, on a dark night on a Cornish cliff, just out of a comfortable bed, floundering in the undergrowth. The dog cried again, and it sounded as if it were at my elbow, and when I got to my feet the torch shone on the dog five yards away beneath a small elder tree. A front leg was strung up high above its head. I could see a thick wire circling the trunk of the tree four feet from the ground, and from this wire sprouted the snare, and the dog had run into it, and it had pulled pincer-tight just above its right paw.

'Hell,' I shouted. 'A badger snare. I didn't know they existed!'

The dog was a beagle hound, and I had never seen it before. It stared at us quite quietly and never for a moment did I think that, out of panic, it might attack me as I tried to release it. Other dogs might have done, but not this one. I sensed it was gentle, and that I could set out safely to do the job.

'Thank goodness, Jeannie,' I said, handing her the torch, 'that you had the idea of bringing the secateurs.'

They were not sharp. They were not wire cutters, and the wire of the snare was a quarter of an inch thick and made up of strands of wire. It was five minutes before I was able to cut through it, and then I had only been able to cut the wire attached to the tree. A length was still attached to the beagle, and there was a horrible lock on it which I found impossible to prise open.

'The only thing to do,' I said, 'is to carry it home and I'll have another try there.'

So we stumbled back the way we came, through the moorland to the lane, up towards the cottage and across Monty's Leap, the beagle becoming heavier and heavier in my arms. The donkeys were where we had passed them before, and the light shone on Fred's quizzy face, and he began again to make a snuffling noise.

'Quiet, Fred,' I repeated.

One glance at the wire in full light was enough to show that I would not be able to release it. An expert was required, and quickly. The dog had been trapped for eight hours or more. We couldn't wait for the morning.

'We'll go straight into Penzance,' I said, 'and I'll ring the vet on the way.'

Thus, at four in the morning, I was standing in a telephone kiosk close to the promenade talking to a sleepy vet, who told me to take the dog to the surgery and a colleague would come round and see to the matter. No grumbles on his part. No doubts that I might be wasting his time. And when the colleague arrived, a young Australian from Queensland, he looked at the snare and said it was diabolical. It took half an hour before the beagle was finally freed.

We took it back to Minack after that, and gave it a meal and a bowl of water, and made a bed for it in the greenhouse. Later in the day, a harassed gentleman arrived, saying he had lost a beagle and had we seen one? 'Oh yes,' I said, and took him to the dog and watched the reunion.

But what would have happened to Nonny, as we learnt was her name, if we hadn't heard her barking? True, she ought not to have been on the land in the first place, but there had been no public notice that badger snares were in the neighbourhood. And supposing it had been a badger instead of a beagle? How long would it have suffered?

I rang the Ministry of Agriculture at Truro and they admitted that snares (and there were others besides the beagle's one) had been set under their auspices. The 1973 Badger Act, aimed at preventing badger persecution, I was told, did not apply to the Ministry. . . .

First Oliver in a rabbit snare, then the beagle in a badger snare. I was glad we were able to help both of them

I had, of course, made resolutions on other New Year Days. All of them had soon fled away out of sight; all of them, that is to say, except the one which concerned Martha.

Martha is the help in the cottage. Martha is responsible for the cleaning, dusting and Hoovering. Martha is furious if anyone forgets to wipe the mud off their shoes before coming into the cottage, or if anything is spilt on the carpet. Martha shakes the cushions on the sofa, removes untidy newspapers, sees that the scuttle is full, carries away the ash from the fire, removes any cobweb in a ceiling corner, dusts the frames of pictures. Martha, if in a good mood, is an admirable servant. Martha was born of a New Year resolution. Martha is me.

Martha was first created by A. P. Herbert on one of the occasions he was staying with us. He had sympathy for the biblical Martha with all her comings and goings; and he had an admiration for Jeannie's conscientious activities of cooking, looking after the cottage, and earthy work in the fields. Thus Jeannie became the first Martha at Minack, and A. P. H. gently praised her with a song called 'When I'm Washing Up', set to music by Vivian Ellis in *The Water Gipsies*, that A. P. H. wrote at Minack. Later, outsiders helped in the cottage and, although each one at the time eased the tediousness of Jeannie's routine, there were also disadvantages. We were not independent. We had to organise the day to suit the help; and when at last Jeannie and I decided to care for the cottage on our own, I celebrated by buying from an antique shop a small Bristol glass hand-bell. We call it the Freedom Bell, and periodically I ring it just to remind us how pleasant it is not to be under an obligation to anyone.

After my New Year resolution to take my share of the housework, after I had proved to be serious about doing so, Jeannie began to call *me* Martha. A silly game, though a game that turned tiresome chores into those of amusement. Like Jeannie saying: 'Martha, you haven't hoovered the carpet today.'

I do not mind her catching me out. Only when I was young did I believe there was a virtue in having someone looking after the place where I lived. I once thought of myself becoming a kind of Bertie Wooster, with an amiable servant to tolerate my eccentricities; a rich young man who was cosseted by his servant. But I was never rich, and never had such a servant, though when I had my first flat in London in Elm Park Garden Mews close to the Kings Road in Chelsea, there was the wonderful Mrs Moon who cleaned the flat. She doted on me, was tolerant of my misbehaviours, was ecstatic at seeing my name in large letters on the sides of London buses at the time when I was writing a column in the *Daily Mirror*; and, after her first visit to the countryside, she swore she would never go again because the silence frightened her. The Luftwaffe over London, on the other hand, did not frighten her to the same extent. 'Old 'itler won't get me down,' was a remark she made. Mrs Moon was an historical Londoner. London was her being.

There were others who tended me. Mrs Youdall was married to a chauffeur who drove gilded young ladies to their débutante dances. Mrs Chevins came for one day and never returned. Mrs Benson was housekeeper when I lived in Richmond, and her chief merit was the marrows she cooked, stuffed with minced meat and herbs. I was fond of Mrs Benson, but she left a curious memento after packing her bags and marching out one day. I found a dead bat hanging in her cupboard. There was Mrs Clarke, who was with me when I married Jeannie, and who tormented us after the marriage ceremony by insisting on walking close beside us as we walked down the path from the church door to the car. 'Go away, Mrs Clarke!' I was spitting, while the photographers clicked their cameras. 'Go away!'

Then there was the elderly lady who was a thief, though I never caught her in the act. Small articles disappeared, small change. At last came the moment of embarrassing circumstantial proof. I had a number of guests for a cold Sunday lunch, Poles, Yugoslavs, American journalists and a prominent Communist and his wife. Before lunch, we adjourned to a neighbouring pub, leaving the house empty save for the elderly lady concerned. When we returned, the pretty wife of the Communist looked for the handbag she had left behind in the drawing room. She found the handbag, but the contents were missing. Eight pounds.

At Minack, however, we do not have parties. Indeed, we are anti-social in the sense that we have little wish to be guests in other people's houses and we seldom invite people in advance to Minack. Advance invitations demand of you so much in self-conscious preparation; and so, by the time the guests are due to arrive, I find myself at the window, alternately looking up the lane or looking at my watch, wondering how late they are going to be, and in a mood that inclines me to regret that our invitation has ever been made.

We prefer the unexpected visitors, those on our wavelength who have suddenly decided to take the trouble to see us and arrive, not knowing whether we are here. It happens quite often. It has a pattern. They may arrive around mid-day and we offer them a glass of wine, and by one o'clock they are murmuring about leaving so that 'you two can get on with your work'. We offer them another glass, and with a show of reluctance they accept ('half a glass, please') . . . and an hour later they are delving into the pâté, cheese or whatever else that is available. The advantage of such an occasion, or of any occasion which has not been pre-fixed, is that no shadow has been thrown over the previous hours. Martha has had no domestic work to do in preparation. Jeannie hasn't had to worry what clothes she ought to wear, or what lunch she should give. The guests are treated as birds of passage. The occasion is uncomplicated. It is fun.

Sometimes, of course, the unexpected guest can cause a problem.

We had a gentleman with a high-pitched voice, who would take the bus out from Penzance, walk down the mile-long lane and present himself at our door just as I was about to settle down to cheese, biscuits and William Hardcastle's *World at One*.

We welcomed him the first time. We yielded to him the second time. The third time, a week later, we were lucky enough to spy his dapper figure crossing Monty's Leap, and we escaped through the back door into the wood, where we hid, listening to the high-pitched voice enquiring of Geoffrey where we were. We thought we were safe, and it would have been so if it had not been for Fred. At that very moment, in Houdini fashion, he succeeded in unlatching the gate of the stable meadow. Geoffrey saw him do it, and we heard him shout . . . 'The donkeys are out!'

A minute later, our unwanted guest saw us dash out of our hiding place and run up the lane and beyond. He had caught us. We had still to catch Fred.

We do not often have people to stay, and when we do, if it is a couple, we move out of the cottage and sleep in the one-time stable which is now my office, and the couple have our bedroom. We moved out for George and Sophie

Brown when they came to stay with us not long after he had resigned from being Foreign Secretary. We had become friends when he stayed at Lamorna before the 1964 election, and we used to meet again periodically in the ensuing years when we went to London. He had now invited himself for five days, and the prospect alarmed us. Five days with a turbulent George Brown in a small cottage, a mile off the road, and without a telephone could be explosive. Nor did the day of his expected arrival augur well.

At mid-day we received a telegram: 'Very sorry. Must cancel visit.'

This was a let-down. Preparations galore, and now a void. We felt sorry for ourselves until tea-time. Then another telegram arrived: 'On our way. Arriving midnight. Much looking forward to holiday.'

'What's the reason, I wonder, for all these changes of mind?' I said.

'Sophie,' Jeannie said. 'I expect Sophie has persuaded him after all.'

Sophie Brown is a gentle person, tolerant, kind and easy to be with. Jeannie says she is the kind of woman that other women always like to have as a friend.

'How are we going to stay awake?' I asked. We always go early to bed. It is the Cornish air. It is sleep-making.

'Matchsticks,' said Jeannie, laughing.

This was the joke which was produced whenever there was a need for us to stay up late. It began when I was writing a book about the British Empire and I had to work into the early hours of the morning. I used to say that I kept awake by keeping my eyes open with matchsticks.

At midnight—it was the end of July—we positioned ourselves at a spot above the cottage beside the well and stared northwards to where we would first be able to see the lights of a car coming along the lane from the main road.

An hour went by, and the lane remained in darkness; and then at last we saw a smear of light, and we watched it coming nearer and nearer, the smear growing larger until it reached the farm buildings at the top of the lane, when the smear turned into headlights before it began to descend our lane, and then the headlights turned into a smear again because of the high hedges.

'He's travelling very fast,' I said, nervously.

'He's remembered the way,' said Jeannie, 'and I expect he's thankful the journey's over.'

The car had now reached the turn at the far side of Monty's Leap so that the headlights shone directly towards the cottage. There was no slackening in its speed.

'I'm a bit scared,' I said, joining Jeannie in hastening down the path to the space beside the barn covered with stone chippings where all cars had to stop.

The car had now leapt Monty's Leap. It was heading straight for Jeannie.

'*Stop*, George,' I heard her call out.

And the car stopped.

It was a police car.

George Brown had had a collision at an Exeter roundabout ('*not* my fault' he explained later) and he had asked the police to let us know that the car had to be repaired, and he was staying the night in Exeter, and would not be arriving at Minack until late in the afternoon.

'Thank you very much for your trouble,' I said to the two police officers.

'Great chap, George Brown,' said one.

'He's honest,' said the other one. 'That's what one likes about him.'

Arriving late in the afternoon . . . the snag was that we were opening the Lamorna Fête that afternoon with Penny and Fred. This alone was trouble enough for one afternoon. We had to walk Penny and Fred to the field beside the Lamorna road; we had to persuade them to enter the field, and we had the responsibility of giving rides to dozens of children. It was a worrying prospect, and now there was the additional worry that the Browns, in a battered car, might arrive in our absence. Jeannie, therefore, left the Fête early, leaving me to take the donkeys home on my own.

We were half-way up Boleigh Hill, the donkeys and I, when there was a toot on a horn, and a Jaguar with a battered front drew up beside us.

'George!' I called out, with pleasure, and Fred immediately shied to my right . . . 'Welcome!'

It was a solemn George, a solemn Sophie. Hardly a smile. Hardly a greeting.

'Jeannie's waiting for you,' I said, cheerfully. 'You remember the way? Turn left by the milkstand, then up the lane with the barn on your left!'

They moved off, and I watched them disappear up the hill.

'Come on, you two,' I said to the donkeys, pulling at their halters. 'Hurry up . . . we have got a lugubrious ex-Foreign Secretary on our hands, and you'll have to help in dealing with him.'

I have sometimes felt envious of men of power because life must be simpler if you know exactly where you want to go, what you want to achieve. Men of power are not fogged by contradictions within themselves. Their ambition is as clear as the moon on a summer's night. They want to control their fellows. They want the obedience of the mass. They want applause.

But did George Brown ever possess the real, biting ambition for power? I do not believe so. Events pushed him; he did not push himself. His heart was too big to allow him to be cunning, and men of power have to be cunning if they are to survive. He was aware of this weakness, if it were a weakness, within himself, and it was the cause of his celebrated outbursts. He was shouting in the dark. He was raging against the fates which offered him prizes which other men longed for, but which he, basically, did not feel able to accept. The public sensed this and loved him for it; still do for that matter. A man with a heart is always likely to be more loved than an intellectual.

'Oh, George is tired,' said Sophie that evening. 'Oh, he's tired. This is his first holiday for four years.'

The evening was easier than I expected. Easier, I believe, than George expected. He thawed with the help of a glass or two of La Guita sherry, a good dinner from Jeannie, and a bottle of wine; and we finished the evening with Jeannie and Sophie talking at one end of the room, while George and I sat at the other end, listening to records of Callas and Stephano in *La Bohème*, George extravagantly performing the motions of a conductor.

The following morning the cottage curtains were still drawn at ten o'clock. I had already been to Newlyn to buy mackerel and the newspapers. While I was there, I met a die-hard Conservative.

'I hear you've George Brown staying with you,' he said.

'News certainly travels fast.'

'I hope you shoot him.'

Nobody emerged from the cottage until eleven o'clock. It was then that I was startled by a curious noise coming from the donkey field just above the cottage garden. I hurried up the path to have a look and, as I drew near, the noise rose to a crescendo . . . and when I turned the corner I saw the cause of it. George, in open-neck sports shirt on this sweet summer morning, was still in a Puccini mood, and he was singing into the skies *Your Tiny Hand Is Frozen*. That was not all. Fred, close to him but above in the field, was also singing. Fred always appreciates a chance to hee-haw and the louder George sang, the louder was his hee-haw. Up and down the scale, head pointing to the heavens, clear notes, tremolo notes, hysterical notes. . . . Fred was countering George's baritone with a tenor-like bellow.

George saw me.

'Ah,' he said. 'I've made a friend!'

'How did you sleep?'

'First time I've had a full night's sleep in years.'

'Glad of that,' I said, relieved.

Shortly afterwards I handed him the newspapers I had brought back from Newlyn. He glanced at the front page of one of them.

'Damn lie. I never said that. Pure invention. . . . .'

He was still at the time Deputy Leader of the Labour Party and there were those who were pushing him to resign. He was intending to resign, it seemed to me, but he wasn't going to be manoeuvred into resigning by intriguers. No bile, however, on his part. I heard him speak criticism of some of his colleagues, but there was never a word of viciousness.

The weather was fine all through the five days. He sat often on the bridge, as we call it, facing the sea and the wide sweep of Mount's Bay. Directly in front of him was a small bed of mignonette, where bees hummed and settled on the serrated little flowers.

'Look,' he said. 'The bees have red socks' (the bees having touched the pollen). 'Good socialists obviously.'

We were in tomato time. Geoffrey picked the tomatoes three times a week, carrying them into the packing shed, grading them, and then driving the chip baskets to the wholesaler in Penzance.

'You're packing them wrong, Geoffrey,' said George one morning. Geoffrey now had the advice of the man who once had the responsibility for the economic affairs of the United Kingdom, the man whose Declaration of Intent foreshadowed the Social Contract.

'How?' said Geoffrey. Geoffrey was often blunt.

'Back the car,' said George, 'so that the rear is at the packing shed door. You're wasting minutes of your time loading the car with the bonnet facing the shed.'

Geoffrey obliged.

I asked him later what he thought of George.

'Seems a nice enough chap,' he replied.

We never left the environment of Minack during their stay, except once when I took George down to the Wink at Lamorna. It was not a success. George was in one of his silent moods, monosyllabic answers, pursed lips, a bit scaring. There was no one to spark him in the pub.

He preferred to stay at Minack. Late waking up, a mackerel breakfast, a stroll, a talk with Penny and Fred, lager at mid-day, teasing of Jeannie.

'Are we having runner beans tonight? Let me help you pick them. Let me shred them.'

He had a passion for fresh runner beans.

Jeannie said to him one afternoon:

'Why don't politicians guide people into realising that the true values of life are free like the sun, kindness, seeing the best in other people's natures . . . instead of always insisting that materialism is the key to happiness?'

He waggled a finger at her.

'My dear, politicians cannot promise the public other than money because they would receive no votes. If politicians advocated the kind of pleasures you find pleasure in, simple pleasures, the public would say it was a dodge to cheat them out of the next wage rise.'

Another time; another question.

'What is this perfect life,' I asked, 'that politicians are always promising us? A sort of mass playground?'

I knew too well that one had to be on guard when asking him a question. Ask it in the wrong tone and he could explode.

But he answered gently:

'In time, the new society will learn to enjoy the subtle pleasures of life. It will take time. One has to be patient.'

'And, meanwhile,' I said, somewhat boldly I realise in retrospect, 'the more people are promised, the greedier they become, and the more violent they are ready to be to satisfy their greed.'

I waited for his reply, but he said nothing. He was staring moodily in front of him. Then suddenly:

'What you need in West Cornwall is a balanced new town. You don't want all these retired people cluttering up the place. You need a reason to keep the young here. What are the youth migrant figures in Cornwall? If I were in office I would send for them.'

'But, George,' I said. 'What's wrong with retirement? Why do planners always make retirement sound as if it were a dirty word? These people have worked hard all their lives to be happy for the last years of their lives . . . and they spend their pensions and savings in the area. They are as useful as any imported industry and without doing any harm to the environment . . . and much more useful than the multiple stores who take their money out of the county.'

Again he did not reply.

His mind had wandered. He was no longer listening to me. He would have replied to me with invective had he been in the mood.

Another time:

'I'm so relaxed,' he said, 'that here I am looking out to sea, listening to sounds, watching small things.'

'Like the bees with red socks,' I said, 'who are Socialists.'

Strange, I thought, that when he first came to Minack the great Offices of State lay ahead of him, and there had been in him a great, driving hope for the future. He had been turbulent then, determined to act, an evangelist with clear-cut solutions. Notable occasions were awaiting him. Meetings with de Gaulle, Willi Brandt, Lyndon Johnson, Kosygin, Nasser, Mrs Golda Meir, all the great figures of that era. The destiny of the British people could be influenced by him. He could win the applause of the United Nations. He could lead us into the Common Market . . . and now, as he looked at the bees, what had been achieved?

45

The Common Market, yes. That was his greatest achievement.

'One day you'll be back,' I said.

'Resigning politicians never come back,' he replied.

'Churchill did.'

'Ah, he needed a war.'

'You both have a common denominator. You both had violent opposition within your own parties . . . and you both had a charisma with the public.'

He looked glum, pursed lips again. No wise man asks George further questions when he is in that mood.

Minack had soothed him, I think that. When he left, I heard by chance a remark he made. I wasn't meant to hear it. I was about to carry his suitcase out to his car, now repaired, when I saw him turn suddenly back. He was making a sentimental gesture.

'Goodbye, little bedroom,' he was saying, 'goodbye.'

A man with a heart, I said, is more likely to be loved than an intellectual. The trouble about intellectuals is that they live in a rarefied atmosphere. Watch them discoursing on television and you find their attitude to humanity is that of a theorist, something to argue about, but never to analyse if it conflicts with a pre-conceived opinion. Intellectuals are seldom generous-minded. They like to find faults in other people's efforts, real or imaginary, and to debase the achievements of their fellows. They are very glib. They do not seek what is best in people or in their work. They do not accept simplicity as a virtue. Truth is something to be knocked, they will steer away from it, clouding it with complications. For the most part they are *poseurs*, pretending to live a life of wit, charm and knowledge, when all that is happening is that they haven't the courage to face their true selves. The most terrible experience of an intellectual, for instance, is to meet someone who is happy.

One such person, a distinguished, world-weary intellectual, came to Minack not long after George Brown's stay.

I listened to his comments on world politics, his sweeping generalisations as to why America was doing this and Russia doing that, what was wrong with this politician and that author, what the government should do, and so on. Then, in a gap of his conversation, I began to talk about ourselves. He listened patiently for a while as I explained the kind of life we led. Then suddenly he exploded, and he turned to his wife:

'Good God,' he said, in a tone that suggested I had insulted him. 'These two are *happy*!'

Occasionally, very occasionally, we have that formal lunch party we prefer to avoid. One day, we received a letter from the editor of *Gourmet* Magazine in New York, the sophisticated American food and travel magazine, saying that she was coming to Cornwall and would like me to write an article about Minack. Lunch was arranged. Jeannie developed a build-up of apprehension (what do you give the editor of such a magazine to eat?), while Martha worked overtime making the cottage a joy to behold.

I met the editor at the Queens Hotel in Penzance to avoid the likelihood of her losing her way in trying to find Minack; and when I arrived I found, instead of the formidable business lady I expected, a soft, soignée, very attractive New Yorker called Jane Montant; and she had accompanying her a photographer, Ronny Jaques, who travelled the world for *Gourmet*, a marvellously evocative photographer as I now know, and who reminds Jeannie and me of Bob Capa, the *Time* and *Life* Magazine photographer, legendary pursuer of wars, who was killed in Vietnam. Bob Capa was with us the night our home in Mortlake was bombed. I can see him now at the half-opened front door, a cigarette languidly dangling in a corner of his mouth, counting the stick of bombs as they fell towards us: 'One, two, three . . . *now!*' I could also see Ronny Jaques behaving as nonchalantly in the same circumstances.

47

I brought these two back to Minack, and Jeannie gave them her carefully thought out lunch . . . fresh crab and her own special mayonnaise, followed by thunder and lightning (treacle tart and Cornish cream), or alternatively hazelnut flan with raspberries, and there was cheese, of course, and wine.

We finished the lunch and they showed no signs of wishing to leave. Nor did we ourselves want them to do so. It is one of the advantages of living in an isolated cottage where there is no telephone, no sudden ring of a bell to interrupt a flow of conversation, that time passes by without being aware of it. Conversation roams on, arguments and views are expressed, and wrong impressions corrected at leisure. Such occasions create friendships in a few hours which otherwise might take years.

A copy of *Gourmet* is now sent to us every month and, since that lunch, we have often been with Jane Montant and Ronny Jaques; and we have written other articles for *Gourmet*, including, by Jeannie, articles on the Savoy, the new Berkeley Hotel and Claridge's. And it was a recipe from *Gourmet* that sent me off to fulfil my New Year resolution to become a cook.

I had been sitting in the cottage looking through the most recent issue when Jeannie arrived back from a visit to Penzance.

'A wonderful *Gourmet* issue this month,' I said.

Jeannie paused.

'Containing more recipes for me to follow, I suppose.'

'Not only you.'

'Don't tell me you're going to fulfil your cooking resolution.'

'I am.'

'Heavens . . . what's it to be?'

'Onion soup,' I said.

'I don't believe you.'

'Why?'

'Onion soup, well . . . it's so ordinary!'

48

'Not the way I'll prepare it. My onion soup, you'll find, is a great delicacy.'

Jeannie looked at me, doubtfully.

'We'll see,' she said.

FOUR

'I'll need your help.'

'But it's *your* onion soup.'

'Well, there are just one or two items . . .'

'Such as?'

'I must have two pints of stock.'

'Surely you know how to make that?'

'Not absolutely certain.'

'I've both beef and chicken stock cubes. Which is it to be?'

'Chicken,' I said, decisively. I hoped I was correct. The *Gourmet* recipe made no mention of chicken or beef stock. It just said stock. Two pints for four portions.

'I also need,' I continued, 'one and a half ounces of butter, a tablespoon of flour, salt and pepper, and a bayleaf.'

'Now, Derek,' Jeannie said, patiently, 'the idea was for you to make this onion soup, and yet you are expecting me to do all the preparing.'

'Certainly not. All I'm asking is for you to give me the ingredients, and then I'll do the rest. I've already got the onions.'

We grow onions. We used to buy them from a Breton onion seller who called twice a year, and who came from Camaret on the Brittany coast where live a number of people with the name of Tanguy. The Tangye family originally came from Brittany and my father wrote a booklet in which he tried to trace its background. He based his research around the Tannegui du Chatel family, whose ruined château still exists at Kersaint in Finistère. One of these, Guillaume, was killed in a naval battle with the English and, to avenge his death, his brother Tannequi, Chamberlain to Charles VI, Provost of Paris, and who fought at Agincourt, came to the west of England in 1404 'with 400 men at arms and wrought much damage on the English in the course of two months' stay, after which he returned to Brittany laden with heavy booty'. My father gently suggested that he met a Cornish lady during his stay and that she was the mother of John Tayngy, the first recorded name similar to Tangye. My father also traced a Saint Tanguy, although he was unable to record the gentleman's saintly virtues.

'So if you'll give me these ingredients,' I went on, 'I'll take them down to the field kitchen and get on with the job of chopping the onions. And, oh yes, I want a large saucepan and another for the stock.'

'You're sure you wouldn't like to go for a walk, and let me make the soup instead?'

'Don't be unfair.'

The field kitchen is in the small greenhouse close to the cottage, in a meadow circled by elm trees with a view of the sea in the distance. It is here that we bunch daffodils in the spring and grade tomatoes in the summer. It serves other purposes as well, such as being a dumping place for a variety of things which I cannot make up my mind whether to keep or not, and for old newspapers galore containing articles I intend to cut out, but never do . . . and as a field kitchen.

This field kitchen was my idea, inspired by Oliver and Ambrose or, more accurately, by the smell of their fish in the cottage when it boiled on the electric stove. Why, I thought, do we not install camping equipment in the greenhouse so that we could be spared the stink? I thereupon acquired a calor gas cylinder and a double burner and, from that moment, the greenhouse endured the stink instead; and it also became the scene of other cooking, messy cooking for the most part, like the making of tomato purée . . . and now of onion soup.

Oliver and Ambrose, however, believed that whatever the culinary activity in the greenhouse, the result was always to be meant for them. Hence, after the burner was lit and the contents of the saucepan began to simmer, they would mysteriously respond to the delicious aromas by suddenly appearing, and behaving in that special cajoling fashion which is the habit of cats when anticipating a feast . . . walking round in circles, arching of the back, a quite unnecessary rub of the head against the leg of a chair. This ritual was understandable when fish was in the saucepan. It made them look foolish when the saucepan was filled with stewing tomatoes . . . or onions.

Ambrose was about to look foolish.

I had been standing for a few minutes at the bench chopping the onions, the stock saucepan on the burner beside me beginning to warm, when Ambrose appeared in the doorway. He paused for a moment, gave a squeak, then hurried past me with tail in the air, and jumped on the bench a few yards away. Again a squeak.

'Idiot,' I said, puffing at my pipe. 'What an idiot you are to think you would like onion soup.'

I was contemplating, as I spoke, how effective a shield the pipe smoke was against the tear-jerking effect of onions. Perhaps I had made an important culinary discovery. No tears in my eyes as I chopped. No tears in any housewife's eyes if she puffed at a pipe. A tip, I lightheartedly said to myself, that I must pass on to Jeannie.

Squeak . . . squeeeek . . . a prolonged squeak.

'Idiot,' I said again.

I continued to chop the onions while he stared at me. Dark ginger stripes between his ears, dark ginger shapes on his body resembling miniature shapes of clouds in the sky, a small, white shirtfront, white whiskers and a pink nose, a plush tail with ginger circles, pale ginger paws. His similarity to Monty and Jeannie's paintings of Monty which hang in the cottage was becoming more remarkable every day as he grew larger.

Squeak.

This squeak was Ambrose's signature tune. He squeaked instead of miaowing, an absurd noise like a mouse in trouble. He might be sitting on the green carpet of the cottage, keeping his distance, when Jeannie emerged from the kitchen with his supper . . . squeak! Or, I might meet him outside and have a passing word with him, and again he would reply with a squeak. It was a juvenile sound. I had compared it to that of a boy's treble, and thought he would grow out of it. He had not done so.

Squeak.

Neither of us had yet come to terms with Ambrose, nor he with us. If, for instance, I had moved from my onion chopping towards him, he would have scampered away. He would never allow himself to be picked up, nor to be stroked, and it would certainly never enter his head to jump on a lap. At this period of his life, he treated affection as a nuisance. Only sustenance was required of us.

Squeak . . . squeeeeek.

I had by now placed the butter in the second saucepan, and it was beginning to sizzle and to froth, and so I gathered up the chopped onions in my hands and dropped them in. On the one burner the cooking onions, on the other stock coming to the boil. And in came Oliver.

He arrived in the manner of someone late for a party. He hurried in through the greenhouse doorway, paused at my feet, making the sound of his own particular signature tune which is a strangled cry reminding me of the yap of a small dog, and then proceeded to circle round and round one of the legs supporting the bench, rubbing his head against the wood. He too anticipated a feast.

'I thought you were an intelligent cat, Oliver,' I said.

There are some, of course, who decry the habit of those who talk to animals. Silly, sentimental nonsense, they claim it to be. They may even suggest it is a weakness of the brain on the part of the person who does so. Reason may support them because it does seem eccentric to talk to something which cannot answer back. Yet, is the vapid chatter between two people any more sensible?

'Oliver,' I went on, 'you and your son are potty.'

He had now jumped on the bench and, after a head rubbing head welcome with Ambrose, he approached the saucepans. Sniff, sniff, sniff . . .

'Stupid boy,' I said, quoting Captain Mainwaring's frequent remonstration to Pike, then adding a remark of my own. 'Is it really true, Oliver, that you cannot tell a fish from an onion?'

His reply, if it were meant for a reply, was to retreat to the lemon tree, branches of which now covered the far end of the bench, and where Ambrose was already crouched, staring at me; and there the two of them remained, huddled side by side, green leaves around the two cats waiting for a feast they were doomed never to receive.

The lemon tree had been grown from a pip by Jeannie's mother in her Kensington flat, and Jeannie had brought the seedling to Minack after her mother had died several years ago, and had planted it direct into the soil in the corner of the greenhouse. It thrived, and there came a memorable summer when there were flowers on the branches, and in the autumn they began to change into fruit, and by January they were bright yellow lemons; and I was able to say to Beverley Nichols, who was paying us a visit:

'Would you like a lemon with your gin and tonic?'

'Yes,' he replied.

'Come and chose your own lemon,' I was then able to say. We had more than a dozen bright yellow lemons that year . . . but since then not a flower, not a lemon. Only a profusion of lemon-scented green leaves on spiky branches which reach to the greenhouse roof.

We have, however, set out to find what is at fault, and whenever a gardening expert visits us we ask for advice. We learnt, for instance, that we had made a fundamental mistake. We had pulled the lemons off the tree instead of cutting them . . . for it is essential to leave the 'button' intact at the apex. It became clear also that we had failed to prune sufficiently because all weak shoots, all old and bare wood, all long branches, should be cut from the tree. Then there was the condition of the soil, and although it was rich and we kept it well watered, we were told one day it lacked one essential ingredient: wood ash.

Our informant was the noted garden expert Shewell Cooper, who breezed into Minack during a tour of the West Country. An extrovert, large and boisterous, he succeeds by his enthusiasm in making the solution of all gardening problems appear to be as simple as adding two and two together. He is an apostle of organic growing, and he is responsible for the Good Gardeners Association, whose headquarters at Arkley Manor, near Barnet, provide a practical demonstration of what organic growing can achieve. He is against all forms of chemical fertilisers, believes compost can provide most of the manure a garden requires, and that in a well-balanced soil the worm population is sufficiently active to take the place of hand digging and cultivating. His rhetoric is persuasive on these matters. He once lectured at a meeting in Bradford and, a year later, he received a solicitor's letter from that city. 'If you are the person,' the letter read, 'who lectured on compost a year ago, I have good news for you. A lady who was present has left £1,000 to you in her will.'

He looked, therefore, at our sterile lemon tree and declared: 'Wood ash round the roots, that's what's needed. Wood ash will work wonders . . . also some pruning.' He proceeded to do the pruning himself. 'That advice is worth five pounds,' he said, laughing, his shoulders heaving.

As soon as he had left—it was evening time in late summer—I observed Jeannie set off into our copse-size wood with a basket; and in due course she returned with it full of small broken branches. Then she went off again, then again, until there was a pile of broken branches available for a fire. Our Courtier stove in the sitting-room had been unused since the spring. It was now to become active for the sake of a lemon tree.

Unfortunately, Jeannie had made a miscalculation. I, too, for that matter. I had watched her stuff the stove with wood, watched her light it, and had been totally blind to what could be the result.

It was a delightful soft summer evening, and I went up to the bridge for a drink. The bridge which isn't a bridge, but provides the effect of a ship's bridge as one stands there, gazing out across Mount's Bay to the Lizard . . . I was standing there, facing the moorland and the sea, when I observed thick smoke emerging from the chimney. It is a small granite chimney, square, and on cold winter days Philip the gull, or Flotsam and Jetsam, the other two gulls who regularly visit us, like to sit there warming themselves. The chimney has also played its part in the sea annals of Mount's Bay because fishing boats, as they came into the Bay heading for Mousehole, Newlyn or Penzance, used to line up the chimney with the great rock that balances on another at Carn Barges which we see from our windows; and when the Carn and the chimney were in unison, they knew they could turn to their harbours. The chimney stands there, prodding into the sky, a small monument to centuries of history.

After a few minutes the smoke began to thicken into a menacing plume and, because it was a still evening with no breeze to disperse it, the smoke began to drape itself over the roof so that Philip the gull, who had been waiting for a nightcap of a piece of cake, became so uncomfortable that he shuffled his wings and flew off.

I ran down the few paces to the cottage, calling Jeannie,

and into the cottage, and there she was in front of the stove, a pile of broken branches beside her, stuffing them into the now blazing grate.

'Stop it!'

'Why? What's wrong?'

'The chimney's on fire!'

'Rubbish.'

'It is, I tell you!'

Jeannie is single-minded when she gives herself a job, and it is better not to try and interrupt her. But the trouble about this particular job was the possibility that the cottage might catch fire.

'You *must*,' I said, 'stop feeding the fire with those branches.'

'They burn quickly.'

'Too quickly,' I said.

'Shewell Cooper said that the lemon tree needed wood ash, and that's what I'm getting. In a few minutes, I'll have a whole heap of pure wood ash . . . and I'll spread it around the lemon tree.'

'Sure, sure,' I said. 'But in a few minutes we may have no home. Don't you understand the chimney is on fire? If we were in a town the alarm bells would be ringing; neighbours would be rushing to help us. . . .'

'Serious as all that?'

'Yes . . . so *please* stop feeding the fire and come outside and see for yourself what is happening.'

The whole environment around us was now covered in smoke, and our old granite chimney was belching out the stuff as if it belonged to an old-fashioned factory complex.

'You're making too much fuss,' said Jeannie, looking up at the smoke.

'Golly,' I replied, 'what more do you want to happen to realise the seriousness of the situation?'

I could scarcely see the greenhouse, or the barn, or the sea which is normally only obscured by thick fog.

'Calm down,' she said. 'You're over-excited. It is only the chimney on fire.'

'Only. . . .'

I have always been fascinated by fires. One of my earliest assignments as a junior reporter on the *Daily Express* in Manchester was to cover a mill factory fire in the Ancoats area. I was so entranced by the blazing flames that the *Daily Express* had to send out another reporter to discover what had happened to me. I was standing, mouth open, gaping at a wall of fire which was about to lurch a wall of the building to the ground, when there was a tap on my shoulder: 'The editor wants to know whether you're feeling all right.'

This, however, was a personal emergency. I could not feel detached. I could not allow myself to be hypnotised. I had to act.

'I'm going to call the fire brigade.'

The fire brigade was in Penzance and, at best, it couldn't be with us for half an hour. First I had to go up the hill to the Trevorrow farm and use their telephone, then the journey of the fire engine along the winding road would take at least another twenty minutes.

Sparks had now joined the smoke from the chimney.

'Damn the lemon tree,' I said.

'*Don't* get so excited!'

I would have preferred not to be so excited. I hated the prospect of calling the fire brigade. I was subconsciously concerned that the fire engine might charge down Minack lane on an unnecessary errand, that Jeannie's calmness might be justified and that, by then, the fire would be out. True, I was over-excited but, at the same time, I was only too ready to do nothing. I was in favour of Jeannie's calmness. I had no wish to make a fool of myself, or to cause trouble. If *only* the smoke showed signs of diminishing.

'Well?'

'Well what?'

'I thought I was about to see you disappear up the lane.'

'I'll wait another five minutes . . . if there is no improvement, I'll go.'

Jeannie's calmness was deceptive. It was not born of assurance, rather it was born of a sense of guilt. She was responsible for the situation. She lit the fire, built it up . . . and she could best counter this innocent foolishness by appearing to believe that all would be well.

'Look,' she said a moment later, 'not so much smoke is coming out now. And anyhow, *why* are you afraid that a chimney fire might spread to the cottage?'

That was a good point. She was attacking me, not defending herself; and why, in fact, was I so worried? The actual fire was caused by the soot inside the asbestos flue which ran up the length of the massive old chimney. The asbestos would withstand the heat caused by the fire, and so there was nothing in near contact which would cause it to spread. The smoke might look fearsome, but that was all.

'One has to be prepared,' I said, lamely.

'Agree, agree, but you can overdo it.'

I now knew that I was overdoing it. The chimney was still belching, but it was a harmless belch. There was no threat to the cottage. Jeannie was right. I had overreacted. She may have been at fault in setting the scene, but she had now recovered her position. She had proved that I, too, had been foolish. We were equal.

The pity is that the lemon tree did not benefit. The tree had its wood ash, but we never had our lemons.

After half an hour of gently stewing in the butter, the onions had become soft and golden brown, so I emptied the tablespoon of flour into the saucepan and stirred it until it had been absorbed in the juices; and then I picked up the saucepan from the other burner and poured in the stock. At that moment, I saw Oliver and Ambrose advancing towards me across the bench; a pair of greedy cats, who thought it was time to participate. I waved the empty saucepan at them.

'Do try and be sensible,' I said, and they retreated back to the lemon tree.

I am now an experienced maker of onion soup. I have onion soup days during which I make a quantity of onion soup, storing it in containers in the freezer, so that there is always some available when I am in an onion soup mood. But, on this first occasion, when I had no knowledge of what the result of my efforts might be, I had a delightful sense of excitement. I saw a hint of the horizon which chefs seek. I was about to create a subtle delight and I was able to sniff the approaching results of my handiwork. I watched the soup simmer, bubbles fluttering in the centre, and as I waited for the simmering period to be completed, I frivolously remembered the pleasure of other onion soups. Two Parisian onion soups in particular.

I was for a while a ghost writer for Schiaparelli, the legendary dress designer, and I used to go to Paris once a month to collect material from her for the article she was under contract to sign in the Sunday newspaper I worked for. She was a thin, gaunt figure, very elegant, with a severe manner, and I found her a little unnerving. The first time I met her was on one of her visits to London, and I was sent to interview her; and when the results of the interview appeared in the paper, she informed the editor that she was so pleased with it that she would like to write a series of articles, so long as I was the one who ghosted them. I was very young, and I was delighted. I foresaw this lady of fashion introducing me into the mysterious, chic Parisian society about which I was currently reading. Schiaparelli, I half hoped, might do for me what Madame de Guermantes did for Proust.

However, this was not to be. The first time I went to Paris to see her set the tone for my other visits, so each visit was to prove as unsatisfactory as the first. I arrived one morning at the appointed time in her salon in the

Place Vendôme and sat waiting, observing elegant clients come and go, for an hour before Madame was ready to see me. Then I was ushered into her office with a huge desk between me and her, and listened to half an hour of staccato advice as to how young women should dress.

It was good advice. It was advice which still holds good. Her main point was that elegant fashion of whatever period is always basically simple. A flurry of fussy clothes might excite spasmodically from time to time, but such a mood was too brash ever to last very long. Thus I remember her saying that women should base their wardrobes on simplicity, but bring change to such simplicity by having a large variety of accessories . . . handbags, fashion jewellery, belts, shoes, silk scarves, and so on. She was particularly keen on scarves because, she said, they *disguised* often worn suits and dresses.

Our discussion lasted for an hour and when it came to an end I had hoped, or expected, she would ask me what I was going to do in the evening, and that when I replied that I had nothing planned she would say she was having a small party at her home and that she would be delighted if I would attend. I even began imagining, during the course of our discussion, that she might be thinking of me as a Chéri and herself as a Colette; and that, therefore, I was about to enter an exciting, dangerous relationship which also might be instructive. After all, I was very young, and she had specially asked me to come to Paris.

My expectations did not materialise. Instead, as she said goodbye, she briskly informed me that her public relations director would take me out to dinner: an elderly, motherly American who, in due course, I found sitting opposite me at Fouquet's, a solemn restaurant in those days, while I wondered, despairingly, how long my evening with her would have to continue. At last it came to an end and I set off to walk the streets of Paris in a determined mood for adventure, and somewhere in the area of Montmartre I found a girl in a bar and I drank Pernod and then she suggested a tour of the seamier side of Paris, and long after dawn had broken I was sitting with her in a scruffy café in Les Halles . . . drinking onion soup. All around me others were drinking onion soup. I was having my first experience of the national soup of France.

My other Parisian onion soup memory took place years later when Jeannie and I spent a month in Paris together. We began our stay in a penthouse suite at the *Georges V* thanks to Jeannie's Savoy Hotel influence, and that first evening as we sat in the balcony garden looking out over the rooftops of Paris, drinking champagne, we experienced elation . . . a month in Paris and this the first evening! We dined on the Ile St Louis, then on to a nightclub in Montparnasse, and a wandering journey back towards the *Georges V* on foot and, on the way, we found a café with an array of lighted candles in the window. We went inside and there at a table was a quartet of people drinking onion soup. That early morning Jeannie, too, had her baptism of the national soup of France.

My own version was now ready. I switched off the calor gas, took hold of the saucepan in both hands, and set off out of the greenhouse and up the path to the cottage. This was a notable occasion. I had started to fulfil a New Year resolution for one thing and I had, judging from the aroma, a delicious Parisian memory to enjoy for another.

I was halfway to the cottage when I glanced behind me. Two cats, tails up, one nudging the other as they walked, benign expressions of expectation on their faces, were a yard or two behind me.

FIVE

'Delicious,' said Jeannie, after savouring the soup.

'Thank you.'

'You have a natural cooking talent.'

'You think so?'

'I'm sure of it. A soup can be very ordinary. This is exceptional.'

'I'm overwhelmed by your compliments.'

'The flavour is so subtle . . . just think how enthusiastic we would have been had it been served in a restaurant.'

'Oh well,' I said, modestly.

'And now that you have made such a good start,' Jeannie went on, 'I urge you to develop your talents.'

'Always pleasant to be encouraged.'

'You've made a good beginning towards fulfilling your New Year resolutions.'

I looked at her. I sensed there was a snag in this flattery.

'What are you hinting at?' I asked.

'Simply that one soup doesn't make a feast.'

'Of course it doesn't.'

'Well then, what are you going to do about it?'

'Ah,' I said, 'you mustn't push me. I must have time to plan.'

She laughed.

'I know what that means,' she said. 'You'll go on

thinking about that onion soup and live on its memory.'

'You're unfair.'

'We'll see.'

'Anyhow,' I said, 'I won't have time now. Geoffrey thinks the daffodils will be in with a flood by the middle of the week if this weather lasts.'

'You're stalling. The trouble with you is that you have no follow-through. You start something and then lose interest.'

'I haven't lost interest. I just like to take things slowly. You wait until the daffodil season is over.'

'I'll be waiting,' she said, laughing.

Jeannie, however, was right. I can be conscientious and persistent if the task involved is one of necessity, but I am inclined to drift, to behave like a schoolboy uninterested in his subject, if there is no crystal-clear reason why I should perform it. I realise also that I could be more positive in other matters. I sometimes say to myself, for instance, that I should participate in public causes, serve on the committee of this or that worthy organisation, or make the effort to push myself into spheres which might bring me useful advantages. My reluctance to do so, I believe, centres around my suspicion of the motives of some of those who act in this way. Many, of course, are selfless and dedicated, but there are those who treat their involvement in public activities as a method of boosting their own egos. They fussily attend their meetings in an aura of such self-importance that their friends and acquaintances, even their families, are duped into believing they are doing something worth while when, in fact, they are only motivated by self-aggrandisement. Such people behave as if the outer façade is a substitute for reality.

Then there is the example of politicians, union leaders, and other public figures of our society, who have a similar façade. They become so confused by the volume of their work, by the endless contradictory reports on this or that, by pressure groups, by cunningly led minorities, by political manoeuvring, that they give up the attempt to keep in touch with truth. They have no time to do so and, as a consequence, they adopt attitudes, holding on to them whatever the evidence may be that such attitudes are false.

I, therefore, do not cherish the idea of moving out from my miniature world. I prefer to heed the dictum of A. P. Herbert that writers should be read and not heard. I prefer to drift. I prefer to stay as I am . . . except I am aware that, from time to time, I will behave out of character.

Each year when the daffodil season begins we are in the mood of pool investors waiting for the Saturday results. We are always hopeful. We always begin by believing that the combination of circumstances required for a successful harvest will materialise and that, during the few weeks of the season, we will earn the money which we have been hoping for all through the year.

First, however, there are the preparations. We have, for instance, to decide where we are going to market the flowers and, this year, we were changing our tactics. Hitherto we had acted on our own, but now we had joined the local Society of Growers, which had wholesaler connections in all parts of the country.

The Society was not a co-operative in the sense that all the produce it handled was sent to the markets under a single brand name. Each grower continued to send his consignments under his own name, thus conserving his individuality, but he enjoyed the use of the Society's marketing organisation which had its headquarters at Long Rock just outside Penzance. This served as an intelligence centre, and here a grower could find out what price his produce had fetched a short time after it had been sold; and he could compare the prices in the various markets and receive advice as to where best he should allocate his sendings of the day.

Thus I might be advised not to send more than thirty

boxes to Covent Garden, or ten to Derby, or twenty to Southampton, though it was up to me to make the final decision. Then, all I had to do was to staple a card on the lid of each box containing the name of the chosen wholesaler and the destination, and take them to Penzance station. The Society also had the advantage of a contract with British Rail whereby there was a fixed transport charge of 18p per box regardless of where the box was being sent, or the number of boxes in the consignment. An individual sender, on the other hand, was charged different prices for different places and the fewer boxes he sent to each place the higher the charges were per box. Hence an individual sender was always tempted to send a large consignment to a single destination rather than spread it around a number of them.

The theory boys suggest that the principle behind this kind of co-operative is the answer to all grower problems. Thus a number of growers should be joined together in one unit, and then proceed to benefit by the advantages of bulk buying (of containers or fertilisers, for instance), the sharing of equipment, and the sharing of labour. Such an ideal has a delightful appeal to those in Whitehall offices and University colleges. It looks neat on paper. It can be eloquently championed on television. It fits the image of brilliant men, operating behind the scenes, who are able to solve the country's economic problems. The truth is, of course, that the theory boys often do not have practical experience in the things they advise about and confuse dreams with reality. They are academics.

Hence their theories of co-operation, of brotherly love, of the practical advantages of sharing, do not materialise in practice; and a main reason for this is the weather. However skilful the grower, however scientific the methods he uses, God remains always in charge. A long period of rain bogs the ground; warm weather in winter brings on a crop too fast; gales may blacken another; a sudden hard frost in spring may destroy another or,

67

ironically, a spell of perfect growing conditions will probably cause a glut. A consequence of this lottery life is the belief amongst growers that independence is a necessity. If, for instance, a group of growers shared the use of an expensive tractor and there came a gap of fine weather after a period of wet, who would be given the chance to use it when each member of the group required it as urgently as the others? Or, when a crop is to be harvested, how is the available labour to be shared when everyone wants it at the same time? Perhaps in some areas of growing, the organisation of such sharing may be possible, but it will be at the sacrifice of that sense of liberty which the majority of growers and small farmers still cherish. They would have to come under a central authority. They would have to be ordered what crops to grow . . . and in the end they would still be at the mercy of the weather.

The sense of liberty, however, is a deceptive emotion. No one is free today. We are watched by computers, blackmailed by minorities and ruled by envy. We have no spur, as our fathers had, to heighten standards, to explore the subtleties of life, to escape from coarseness. We are enclosed in a society which worships the supermarket, and noise, and treats the charm of solitude as a vice. The odd man out is a nuisance and must be stamped upon. We must all be lemmings. We must hide ourselves in groups, hide our individualities, hide our quest for self-fulfilment. We must learn to accept the notion that it is naughty to desire privacy. We must make ourselves believe that it is anti-social to have saved for years so that we can be ill in a private bed without strangers prying upon us, that such saving is a sin compared with spending the money at bingo. We must adjust ourselves to these attitudes, and be careful not to challenge them. If we challenge them, we will be given a label and our views will be ridiculed. Yet all we are doing is speaking for liberty and for those who have died, sacrificing their lives for liberty:

'Went the day well? We died and never knew
But well or ill, freedom, we died for you.'

The killed did not just die for the lemmings. They died
also for those of us who wish to live as individuals; and
liberty is the power of the individual to follow his own
way of life within a framework of commonsense laws and
conventions. Now, however, the laws have become so
extensive and complicated that only the few can understand
them and so liberty, as our fathers knew it, is fading away.
We can no longer follow our dreams. We need no longer
reach for the stars because there will be no reward in
reaching them. We must conform. We must pretend that
we are all equal in brain power, talent, and the capacity
for hard work. Like the fast ship in a wartime convoy, we
must proceed at the pace of the slowest.

It is a situation, ironically, which suits my idle nature.
I do not have to feel guilty when I do not stretch myself.
I can drift without conscience. I can confine any hard work
to doing just enough to preserve our happiness. I need
no longer aim to earn a bonanza because the bonanza
will not be allowed to stay with me. Ambition, as far as
money is concerned, has been quelled. It is a soothing
emotion.

There is, however, a snag to this comfortable attitude.
I still have to earn a living, and so it is easier for me to
talk about my *laisser faire* behaviour than it is to put it
into practice. I do, in fact, perpetually worry about my
financial affairs and it has been a chronic habit for me to
do so all my life. I cannot keep money, I cannot save; and
when on occasions I have collected a large sum I spend it,
then worry and wonder why it is still not in the bank.
Thus, when the daffodil season comes around, we are on
tenterhooks. During the two months it lasts we hope to
earn between fifteen hundred and two thousand pounds.

I arrived one morning at the Long Rock headquarters of
the Society of Growers.

'Hello, my old cock.'

A Mousehole expression.

'Fine, Ben.'

Ben Green was the impassive, genial, humorous manager of the Society of Growers from Mousehole. I had known him since the early years at Minack when we used to grow potatoes, and I would carry the day's digging in the back of the Land Rover to the Nissen hut in the Marazion railway yard, where the company he then worked for had its headquarters. I would pester him and Ken Lakeman, his colleague, for the price the load might fetch in the market, or I would rage because of the low price of the previous day's load. They were very patient. They understood the frustration of growers, and they would try to calm me by explaining that Pembroke had started digging, or that Jersey was at its peak, or, most dangerous of all, Lincolnshire had begun. Or they might have cheerful news . . . gales had blasted the Pembroke crop, or frost had cut the Lincolns, and the price was picking up. Just the information I wanted to hear, not caring for anyone else's misfortune, and I would hurry back to Jeannie with pleased excitement.

'And what can I do for you?' asked Ben.

Outside in the Long Rock yard and in the shelter of the vast hangar, mammoth lorries with bearded long-distance drivers stood loaded with crate upon crate of broccoli. Soon they would be setting off on their journeys through the night to cities all over Britain, and I always marvel at the organisation that lies behind those journeys. Broccoli cut in the field, carried to a collection point, transported to Long Rock, and then Ben Green and his small staff deciding upon which lorry and to which city they should go.

'The daffs have started,' I said.

'Good, good.'

'Only two boxes,' I said, meekly, thinking of the broccoli and the lorries outside.

'Splendid, Derek,' he said, in a tone which suggested I

had brought in myself a vast load of broccoli. 'Talk to Russ about it. He's the flower man.'

Russ I had also known since our potato days. He was an office boy then, and later a van driver. He was now, as I was to learn during the next few weeks, someone who is unable to terminate a telephone conversation. Thus I would make a visit to Long Rock for the purpose of finding out the prices, and then wait, and wait, and wait, while Russ conducted a conversation with some farmer or far distant wholesaler. On, on, on, would the conversation go with Russ at this end replying in monosyllables while the wholesaler or farmer at the other end poured out his troubles.

Russ was free of the telephone on this occasion.

'Yes, my old cock?'

'Just sent two boxes of Mags to Covent Garden on the train. What's trade like?'

Mags, or Magnificence as they are properly called, are daffodils with a golden yellow trumpet and a soft scent, and they grow in meadows down our cliff, our earliest daffodils.

'A bit dodgy, Derek.'

'But the season hasn't yet begun!'

'A lot of Spalding stuff coming in. Glasshouse stuff.'

Stuff is the word. Once upon a time the first bunch of daffodils in a city florist was the true herald of spring. You bought them out of emotion, conjuring up sunny days in the Scilly Isles and the far west of Cornwall, out of expectation of the coming spring, out of the thrill of having a bunch of natural flowers in your dreary city surroundings. Then along came the business men, who saw the prospect of producing daffodils as if on an assembly line in a factory, and they erected vast areas of glasshouses and filled them with bulbs, forcing them to grow quickly in heat. Spring, in the shape of these *ersatz* daffodils, now begins before Christmas, and the wonderment of the true spring flowers is lost; and after Christmas into January and February they fill the florists and supermarkets, anaemic

71

blooms and spindly stalks for the most part, a short life, and a mockery of the true daffodils which last twice as long.

I was to see them, later in this particular season, in Covent Garden. I was astonished to find that they were picked and packed even before the calyx surrounding the bud had broken so that they had the appearance of grass. We ourselves never pick a daffodil until the bud has begun to bulge because, if one picks it before, the bloom will never grow to its normal size; and this, of course, means going over a meadow several times. The glasshouse growers, it seems, do not bother to do this as it would increase their labour costs so they take everything in one picking session. Hence the grasslike daffodils they send to market.

On my return from London, I sallied forth to Long Rock, found Ben and Russ and another man in the office, and proceeded to give vent to my indignation about such Spalding rubbish. I had spoken for a couple of minutes when I sensed a strain in the atmosphere. Ben was shuffling his papers, Russ was looking out of the window, and the man was glaring at me. He came from Spalding.

We had Carol helping us this spring. We usually have someone from a distance who comes for three weeks or so. We had Fran one year, an Australian girl was was on a world tour, then a New Zealand girl, and now Carol. She was tall and slim with long dark hair and wide eyes, and the glasses she wore suited her. She was a secretary when she first paid a visit to Minack, coming to Penzance for a week's holiday, then walking all the way out to the cottage. She was talented in homely matters like knitting, and making original toys, which parents would pounce upon if they saw them, and sewing, and the pressing of flowers, and making people feel at ease. She was quiet and quick in perception, and she provided the steady background Jeannie and I needed during the stress of the flower season. She had now given up being a secretary and, in a wild wish for independence, she had opened a shop in her village of Awsworth near Nottingham where she sold, helped by her mother, her toy ideas and the results of the sewing and the knitting; and this gave her the independence to come to Minack during the daffodil season.

'How are you doing, Carol?'

'I've done twelve dozen bunches in an hour.'

'Geoffrey says you ought to do seventeen dozen.'

'Ah well, you know what Geoffrey's like.'

Geoffrey, in a cheerful mood, enjoyed being a slave-driver; and in any case he was a fast buncher himself.

The small greenhouse where we bunch has the work-bench looking out to the sea in the far distance, through the circle of elms, and across the moorland. We can stand at the workbench and stare far away as we automatically bunch, finding our minds roaming as we so. It is a mood that dissolves all daffodil seasons into one. Long silences; and then a sudden remark.

'You don't eat enough, Carol,' I said.

She was a vegetarian.

'Enough.'

'If you ate more you would bunch faster.'

'You're as bad as Geoffrey.'

'You'd have more stamina.'

'Rubbish.'

'I don't understand you vegetarians. You make eating a science. You make such a fuss about your proteins, too many or too few of them, that you miss all the enjoyment of good food.'

'We manage.'

'It's so clinical, like sick people who are forced to keep to a diet.'

'He's provoking me, isn't he, Jeannie?'

'Don't take any notice of him.'

Silence again. The bunches pile up on the bench beside each of us and, when there are enough, we gather them up and put twenty into a tin. A round number like that made it quicker for Jeannie when she came to pack. Most varieties have forty in a box.

'I see Broadbent over there,' I said. 'Over by that branch above the woodpecker's hole.'

Broadbent was a jackdaw which I nearly buried a couple of years before because I had thought he was dead. Birds do, unhappily, fly into the panes of the greenhouses from time to time and, on this particular occasion, I found this jackdaw lying on the grass just as we were about to begin a day's bunching. There was blood on his head and his eyes were closed and his body was so limp that there didn't seem any point even to try to revive him. I thereupon found a trowel and a little cardboard box and was about to dig a hole in the ground when, still with no sign of life from the jackdaw, I changed my mind. Instead I took him to a nearby wall and placed him in a crevice between two stones; and then returned to the greenhouse to begin the day's bunching.

At lunchtime, I walked over to the wall, glanced at the crevice and found no jackdaw. My surprise was mixed with the pleasure of having been wrong . . . or had the body been taken away by a magpie, even by Oliver, or Ambrose, or Lama who was still with us at the time? I looked around the immediate vicinity and found no sign of it and then, just as I was going away, I saw movement among the lush green leaves of a campion at the base of one of the elms. It was the jackdaw, trying to hide among them. It was a curious experience, seeing something alive which I had been sure was dead.

In due course, we had him in a box with a wire netting as its front, a box which acted as a sickbay whenever we had a hurt bird, but there was the problem of where to put the box. We would normally have put it in the small greenhouse but, as we were using it for the daffodils, we would obviously scare the jackdaw if we put it there. He would be scared in Geoffrey's hut too if we put it there; and so we decided to leave the box in the open, fixed in the wedge of two trunks of a tree where the jackdaw could rest in natural conditions, and yet be safe from marauders.

Very slowly he recovered. We nursed the wound in his head with the ointment of Exultation of Flowers and, in the early stages, we also dosed him with its liquid. From then on it was a question of feeding him with meal in order to build up his strength. One afternoon he was fluttering in the box so strongly that I realised the time had come to free him, and I did so. The jackdaw, which I had been about to bury with a trowel, flew away into the sky, over the cottage chimney, over the meadows and fields towards Pentewan Cliffs. I always knew he came from there. An age-old colony of jackdaws have their home on that grey, granite jagged cliff. A living echo of centuries of times past.

I never expected the jackdaw to come back. I thought he would be absorbed again in his colony. The Pentewan jackdaws were never the social kind of jackdaw you hear about. They always kept aloof. But Broadbent did, in due course, return to Minack, and he has been here ever since. He squats at one end of the roof while the gulls are at the other, and he competes with them for the bread and other scraps we throw up. He is a shy, lonely bird. I have never seen him with a companion, and he has made no response to my attempts to be friendly with him. He has adopted us, but only in a remote fashion. He is, however, resourceful. The other day, I decided we had kept a carton of pâté too long, and so I took off the wrapper and placed it on the bird table for the birds to peck at. Shortly after I saw Broadbent swoop down, seize the side of the carton in his beak, and fly the whole thing away.

Why did we name him Broadbent? I used to have a close friend, a renowned newspaperman, called Jack Broadbent. Both of us still often think and talk about him . . . but more of that later.

'A bit dodgy,' Russ had said of the daffodil trade when we sent our first two boxes, and 'a bit dodgy' it remained for the whole season. It was too warm for one thing; and, while people were going around saying what a beautiful February the country was having, Jeannie and I and all daffodil growers were cursing the sunny days. We should be used to these warm Februarys by now, we have had four of them in a row, followed by sharp frosts as soon as the early tomato plants, requiring oil heating, have been planted in the greenhouses. Every daffodil grower, therefore, was financially suffering from a surfeit of daffodils when another hazard, a man-made one, made our situation even more difficult. A railway strike prevented the growers from sending their flowers to market at the most crucial period of the season.

Strikes, sudden unofficial strikes, or union top-brass-blessed strikes, are so common that we are brainwashed into accepting them as an everyday feature of life. Everyone is treating everyone else unfairly, and we are so momentarily impressed by the arguments posed by the glib spokesman of the illtreated that we sigh and endure. When, however, a strike hits one's pocket, the mood changes. One is no longer an observer, detached, switching off the television because the strike does not concern one, or skipping the paragraphs about it in the daily paper. You are involved because your livelihood is at stake. Your views sharpen, so does your temper.

On this occasion, there were two simultaneous strikes, an unofficial one of porters at Paddington, who refused to shift the flower boxes, and an official one of engine drivers. I never have any sympathy for the former because with almost annual regularity they stage such a strike at some time of the daffodil season. The engine driver strike, on the other hand, although it stung me into such a fury that I sent a telegram of protest to the secretary of their union, would, in calmer times, have extracted from me some sympathy . . . anyone, it would seem, who has the skill and courage to drive a train at a hundred miles an hour deserves the salary of an airline pilot.

However, if these strikes enraged me and my fellow daffodil growers, we were also full of admiration for those who tried to solve our problems. There was, for instance, the sympathy from the staff of the Penzance station. They have always been sympathetic. I have never been to Penzance station without feeling I am in a pleasant club. Perhaps it is because it is at the end of the line, with a sense of finality where dreams end and reality begins, that it invokes such a mood of comradeship. Perhaps it is because the sea is beside it. Perhaps it is because we all feel involved with each other, whatever our tasks, and feel superior to those who live their lives in envy.

And so, when I arrived at the station and asked if there were a chance of a train getting away, I knew I was among friends. Big Donald, normally jovial, but now very concerned; Sailor, incongruously wearing a scarf and no cap, philosophised on the breakdown of standards; and George Mills, who has known us since the beginning when we used to arrive with a load in our Land Rover OPA 40 with seconds to spare and George calling out: 'Make way everyone, make way . . . here comes the Home Farm!' . . . George would now look sorrowful, aware that the livelihood of Cornish growers was being lost, and murmur: 'It's bad luck, it's just bad luck.' Even Sam (short for Samantha), the station's tabby, was sympathetic. Sam owns Penzance station, owns the trains as well for that matter, and periodically she takes a trip on one and ends up at Crewe or Paddington or Bristol; and a message comes over the railway 'phone that Sam is being looked after until the next train home. Even Sam showed her understanding one day when I was standing on a platform, wondering what to do with the flowers. She, who seldom approaches a stranger, actually rubbed against my leg.

Over at Long Rock they were practical in their help.

'We've got a lorry going to Derby,' Ben Green would say. 'Do you mind Derby?'

77

'Don't mind anywhere,' I would reply.

Lorries, scheduled for broccoli, now had to take daffodil boxes as well. Not good companions. The cardboard boxes were at the mercy of the wooden crates.

'Trouble is, Derek,' said Ben, 'we have to use what lorries are available, and so the markets we send them to will get more flowers than they need.'

Scores of daffodil boxes were heaped around the hangar.

'Hell to the strike,' I said, and marvelled at the calm way with which Ben was dealing with the chaos.

'The lorries leave here around four,' he said, 'so try and bring your loads by lunchtime to give plenty of time for them to be loaded.'

The days went by with this haphazard way of marketing, and the prices got lower, and tempers shorter. Then, at last, the strike was settled and we rejoiced and, although it was now too late to recover our losses, too late ever to expect anything near the turnover we had hoped for, we could now resume the normal method of distributing our daffodils.

That night, the night of the day when the strike had been settled, a ferocious gale blew up from the south. I lay in bed listening, though not worrying about it because we have long become accustomed to ferocious gales. It spat and roared and groaned around the cottage, and I lay marvelling at our good fortune that nature, not humans, was in a rage around us, that the wind thundered, not guns. At such moments one luxuriates in awareness of the real freedom. Nature is the king, not man. Nothing organised is attacking. No computer is smugly playing a trick. The gale blows, and is master.

We were up early next morning, eager to bunch a record number of daffodils so that we could make best use of the ending of the strike. I can take forty-two boxes in the Volvo and, as we would have as many as eighty boxes, two journeys to the station would be necessary.

I set off with the first load, and twenty minutes later I

was there in the yard and saw George Mills standing at the entrance.

'Thank God the strike's over,' I said, cheerfully.

'Yes,' he replied, gloomily, 'but it's going to take some time to get the railway stock back where it should be.'

'Is there trouble then? I mean, aren't the trains running as normal despite the strike being over?'

'Worse than that.'

'Why?'

'The station is out of action. It's the gale . . . the sea has flooded the line between here and Marazion. No train can get there, no train can come here.'

Strangely, I did not mind. I had no feeling of anger or frustration. Nature as an adversary, however cruel its effect, can have a calming quality.

I had a sense of relief that there was nobody to whom I could send a telegram of protest.

SIX

Oliver and Ambrose did not enjoy the daffodil season. The bustle, after a period of winter serenity, upset them. They were vexed, for instance, by the field kitchen reverting to its proper use. Daffodil tins were no substitute for a fish saucepan, and they found it infuriating that chatter, activity and an unreadiness to pander to them now dominated the days.

For Ambrose, this was confirmation that the human race was unreliable. Oliver, on the other hand, was puzzled. What had he done wrong to be so ignored? Why should I hurry past him when he curled upside down on the path in front of me? Why should I not pause and listen to his purrs? What made me shout at him in such an excited way when he was sauntering down the lane just as I was about to rush to Penzance with a cargo of flowers? The shouts, the tone of my shouts, were like those that frightened him when first he appeared at Minack, when Lama was Queen. Daffodil days were not pleasant days for Oliver, and he was glad when they were over. So was I.

It had been a poor season. We had taken only £900 compared with the £1,500 or more we had hoped for when the season had begun. The warm weather and the railway strike had been the cause of this, but I feared there was another underlying reason. Too many daffodils were chasing too few customers, and the big growers, with their streamlined costs of production, were ousting the small growers. The same story, in fact, as the supermarket taking away the business of the corner shop.

However, the season was now behind us and we could take up our slow lives again; and Ambrose could be courted; and Oliver receive the attention he longed for. He had a vulnerable nature, a shy mood about him as if he were still not sure that he had settled in the home of his dreams. Lama, when I look back on her life, was a composed cat compared to Oliver. Lama had come to our doorstep when she was less than twelve months old and so she was very young when she realised she had a home for ever. Oliver was seven and a half, for it was seven and a half years since we had found the little black kitten down the cliff, before he could call Minack his home. There was reason for him, therefore, to feel insecure. Years of wandering, of looking for permanence, prevented him from being able to take Minack for granted. He might be thrown out at any time.

His efforts to please me were touching and, if I went for a stroll, I would find him trotting behind me, a black shadow; and although such a gesture did, in fact, please me it also made me nostalgic. Lama used to walk with me in such a manner. Every path, every meadow had seen her with me in all my moods and, at the time, she had seemed to me to be immortal, as all those we love seem to be. Of course, in this functional age, I should have forgotten her by now. Sentiment, for some reason, is a sin, while the sneer is a virtue. I have never been able to understand why.

Thus, when Oliver came on walks with me, he came as half Lama, half himself, and I found myself being sorry for him that my nature was such that I could not treat him as a personality on his own. I was unable, as many people are able to do, to substitute one animal for another, as if one were substituting one piece of furniture for another piece.

The changeover had to take time. It could not be hurried.

I was, however, at ease with Oliver. He did not make me self-conscious by his presence in the way I was self-conscious in Ambrose's presence. Ambrose had to be flattered, and yet still remained maddeningly remote. Oliver only wanted to be loved. Ambrose was like a teenager experimenting with life. Oliver had suffered and now only wanted peace. Ambrose, at this stage, was a taker; Oliver was a giver. The same labels that can be given to human beings. The givers and the takers.

'I'm going for a walk.'

After breakfast one April morning.

'I wish I could come with you.'

Jeannie was packing the dishwasher.

'Why can't you?'

'I'm waiting for the dough to rise.'

Jeannie's home-made bread was so delicious that Flotsam and Jetsam, and Philip, turned up their beaks when offered the steam-blown bread of a baker's shop.

'I won't be long,' I said.

'You go ahead. I might follow you . . . but, if I've time, I want to write to Tannie. I owe her a letter.'

Tannie was my eighty-nine-year-old aunt who lived happily alone in a flat in Chelsea, absorbed in Walpole, Trollope, the Brontës, and any other cultivated writer of the past; and absorbed also in the present activities of a legion of young people, who were fascinated by the way she listened to them. Later in the year, there was to be a special party to celebrate her ninetieth birthday.

'Don't forget to tell her about Mary Stewart.'

A strange incident had taken place ten days before. I had been rummaging one afternoon through a drawer full of photographs when I came across one of Mary holding in her arms her beloved cat, Troy. Troy had been with her in her Edinburgh home during the years of her rise to fame and she and her husband Fred, now knighted for his public services, were selfless in their love for this beautiful black and white cat. Indeed, Mary, during a nationwide tour of bookshops to boost her lovely book *The Hollow Hills*, insisted on returning home to Edinburgh just for the one day to see Troy because he was ill, and then back she came to London and continued her tour.

Troy was nearly eighteen years old and, therefore, there was good cause for her to make that journey. I, however, had no cause to act so strangely when I picked up the photograph of Mary holding him in her arms. I had never met Troy. I had not seen Mary for three years. Yet, when I picked up the photograph, I had a feeling of great sadness; and I said to Jeannie that I was sure Troy had died. Three days later came a letter from Mary. I had been right. Troy had died in the morning of the day I had picked up the photograph.

I set off on my walk with the intention of taking the coastal path to Carn Barges, and then going inland to the top of the valley in which Lamorna lies. It is a pleasant, up and down walk through gorse-covered land with the gorse in places so high that, even in high summer, you are walking in the shade; and you pass through a copse where, in this particular year, I had heard the first chiffchaff in the second week of March, and you cross a little stream which tumbles speedily towards the sea, then onwards through bracken country and past bramble tendrils which try to sneak across the path so that I always take secateurs with me to cut them back. It is a walk that the donkeys love to take and, when I go on my own, I always feel a little guilty that I have left them behind.

I had, however, only just passed through the white gate which leads to the big field, or Fred's field as we call it, because he was born there one May morning beside a flat rock in the centre, when Oliver rushed past me, then came to a full stop and stared back at me.

'I'm going too far,' I said. 'You won't want to come where I am going.'

I went on down the path to the boundary wall and

clambered over it and, as I did so, Oliver rushed past me again, then came to a stop in a damp patch of the path, around which wild mint grows.

'You won't like it,' I said. 'You'll start miaowing soon.'

I felt a mild irritation that I was about to be cheated of my peaceful walk. A sunny morning, no troubles on my mind, the air full of April scents and gulls' cries, and I was to be baulked by a cat.

Miaow.

'There you are, Oliver. I knew it.'

Miaow, miaow.

I had left him behind beside the wild mint.

Miaow!

It was a foghorn of a miaow. A miaow so demanding in its tone that I knew now that my happy walk was ruined. I had to surrender to him. I had to turn back. I had to walk where *he* wanted to walk.

'You're scared, Oliver,' I said, 'because you're outside your territory."

I turned back, over the boundary wall again, Oliver now silent behind me, and then towards the gate of the Minack cliff, brushing as I went the foliage of the scattered Golden Harvest bulbs. Years before, I had invested in Golden Harvest bulbs, a foolish investment as it turned out because the soil on this bottom part of Fred's field where we had planted them did not suit them. It was too warm in summer, causing the bulbs to rot and die, so that now we only had a few scattered ones left.

I reached the gate, unlatched it, and walked down the rough steps which led to the first meadow. I had lost my mild irritation. I was even grateful to Oliver for steering me back to our own land on this lovely April morning; and I paused for a moment thinking back . . . Lama was a part of this cliff all her life; Monty for seven years. Two cats who had witnessed our endeavours and struggles for survival. And now there was Oliver beside me, the twig of a tail gently switching across his front paws, an air of assurance about him because we had returned to his territory. He was home, like Lama and Monty before him . . . and a few yards below us was the little gap in the rock where Jeannie first saw him, the little black kitten on dry leaves, curled asleep in a ball.

A wren rattled its warning note. Why are wrens so foolish? They are small enough to hide in the undergrowth from any prying eyes, human or animal, and yet they are so easily alarmed that they rattle their warning notes, and so bring unnecessary attention to themselves. Oliver, however, showed no interest. He had been a part of the wild, and he was tolerant of wren eccentricity, and so he continued lazily to flick his silly tail, content enough that he had proved his influence over me.

'Oliver,' I said, 'I'll stop contemplating, and we'll go on down.'

The trouble is that it was so easy to contemplate, to let my mind wander. A soft haze waiting for the sun to break through, no human being in sight, no garish building, no man-made noise, only soothing things to watch and hear. A cormorant was drying its wings on the rock called Gazelle and, a few yards away in the sea, a couple of sea-gulls swayed in the swell. A chiffchaff sounded from the blackthorn to my right, and somewhere behind me a robin sang and was answered by another.

I moved from the first meadow to the second, and paused again. I thought back to the time when we planted this meadow with the bulbs of the Magnificence daffodil and how, three years ago, we conscientiously dug them up and transplanted them elsewhere. It was ironic, I now thought as I stood there, that the bulbs we had trans-planted failed in their new meadow, while the rogue bulbs we left behind had multiplied so that there were now as many as when we first planted the meadow.

I went through the California meadow below, treading carefully because the foliage of the daffodils was beginning to flatten, spreading over the narrow path, making it slippery; and I fleetingly remembered how Jeannie's sister, Barbara, staying with us once at this time of the year, slipped on such foliage and fell and broke her arm. An admirable guest. She never complained.

Oliver was close behind me and, as I passed near the little cave, or gap in the rock, where Jeannie first saw the little black kitten curled asleep on the dry leaves, I wondered whether he would take a look at the spot. He didn't this time, though three months later, one morning when he and Ambrose had accompanied Jeannie and me down the cliff, he dashed to it as if he instinctively remembered it as a place of safety.

He and Ambrose had been playing together, chasing each other in and out of the meadows when suddenly the game became too rough for Oliver, and I saw him dash for the little cave, just as a hunted fox might dash to his earth; and when he reached the cave, and Ambrose still rushed towards him, Oliver stood and spat at him. It was enough to stop Ambrose. The game was over, and Ambrose immediately left the vicinity, making a passing sniff at a pink campion as he went, then finding a sudden interest in an untidy clump of couch grass . . . an imaginary mouse, no doubt.

I went down the cliff path, Oliver still at my heels, until I stopped where the palm tree grows. The first palm tree was planted by me when my mother died, and it grew tall enough for passengers on the *Scillonian*, as she passed to and from the Islands, to notice it; and then, a couple of years ago, the fronds began to brown and I, thinking I was helping the tree, used to pull them off. I realise now that I was not helping it, that I was in fact helping it to lose its strength, though I am still not sure whether this was the cause of its dying. Beetles were eating into the bark, thousands of them, and I reckon they must have been the cause, a kind of Dutch Elm beetle. Anyhow, when it was obvious it was not going to recover, I bought a seedling palm; and now, as I stood beside it with Oliver, it was growing healthily upwards only a few feet away from where the first one grew.

I have a letter from my mother which I have never opened. She wrote it to me from London when I was living on an island two hundred miles away from Tahiti in the Pacific; and it never reached me because I had left the island when it arrived. It was forwarded on to me from one address I had just left to another, and another, until finally it reached me months later after I had returned to England. I remember holding it in my hand for several minutes wondering whether to open it and, in the end, I decided not to do so. My reason, I remember, was because the war had begun and the envelope was a gossamer connection with the halcyon days I had lived on the island . . . the envelope had actually *been* to the island. I, therefore, put it in a drawer and as, during the coming years, I moved from one home to another, I continued to keep it in a drawer. It is here now at Minack. Will I ever open it?

My mother was in the tradition of selfless mothers. She hadn't a care in the world provided her three sons were happy. She helped Jeannie and me in many practical ways when we came to Minack, and I do not believe we could have survived had it not been for her enthusiasm and confidence that we had made the right decision to leave London. We were always short of money, critically short, and my mother, unknown to us, would pay periodic visits to her bank manager to whom she would vividly describe the great job we were doing in producing food for the country, potatoes in fact. She was so persuasive that he would agree to advance money through her account on our behalf; and she would send us the money, hiding the fact that she had borrowed it. My mother loved Jeannie, and never lost faith in us.

Around the palm tree and along the banks surrounding the meadows were clumps of primroses, wild violets and celandines and peering from the green of young stinging nettles was the occasional bluebell. The elders were breaking their foliage, and the harsh branches of the blackthorn were a blur of white. Jeannie has a nineteenth-century book on wild flowers, which tells what wild flowers meant to people of those days.

I did not know, for instance, that in Arabia they used to make sherbet by pounding the flowers of violets and boiling them in sugar, or that they used to cultivate great quantities at Stratford-upon-Avon for medicinal purposes, or that there are six different kinds, including the Dog Violet, the largest (though scentless) of the six. We used to grow commercial violets at Minack, but I never thought of extracting a medicine from them, or of pounding them into sherbet. We grew Governor Herrick and Bournemouth Gem, a variety with a long stalk and fragrant scent, though the variety I have always liked most is the traditional Cornish violet called Ascania. We still have it growing in patches around Minack, but the flowers are too small for a commercial market.

The petals of the primrose and the celandine once upon a time were turned into ointment and used to ease sores. The sticky juice of the bluebell, or wild hyacinth, was put to even more practical effect. In days when very stiff ruffs were worn, the juice was made into starch and used to stiffen linen; and it was also used by bookbinders as a glue to fasten the covers of books.

I knew about the elder; that to have an elder growing near your home keeps the evil spirits away and ensures happiness. Unfortunately, elders are tricky things to keep growing. They have a comparatively short life, twenty years or so, before their sap stops running and the trunk and branches dry up; and then, it is said, you must refrain from the temptation of using the dead branches as firewood because to do so is unlucky. No one, however, preaches doom in regard to the picking of the flowers or the berries for the making of wine, and we make the wine every year.

I prefer the white elderflower wine to the red made from the berries and, with its gentle sparkle, it makes a fine summer wine. Picking the flowers is a ceremony, an exciting ceremony because we take the donkeys along to help us, choosing a sunny June morning after the dew has dried from the flowers, and we come down the cliff to the meadows surrounded by elders, and while we pick, using scissors to cut the stems, the donkeys play games. Fred will rush from meadow to meadow, followed by Penny kicking her heels in pleasure, a hilarious demonstration of happiness that they are free to have such a pleasant change from solemnly cropping grass in a field. Then, as we continue to pick, they will suddenly change their tactics and come rushing up to us and nudge us, or Fred will push his woolly face into the basket of flowers. Part of the pleasure when drinking the wine is to remember how the harvest was gathered.

The sun had now broken through the haze and it dazzled a path on the sea, silhouetting the rocks below me, hiding in darkness the gulls that were perched there, so that I heard them squawking without seeing them. Aeons of time and here was the same scene, the same etched lines of the rocks, the same language of the gulls, the same celandines, rose-pink campions, bluebells, wild violets around me, the same greening of the elder trees, the same white of the blackthorn, the same young ferns, the same bridal sprays of the sweet-scented sea-sandwort on grassy banks. A morning to be aware of one's luck. A morning to shout one's gratitude to the heavens. A morning to sympathise with those on trains and buses crowding into cities, or those passing through the factory gates to join the din of machinery. Here was peace. Here was the ultimate which man seeks. Nothing in a supermarket, nothing which could come from the success of a wage claim, nothing that a millionaire could buy, nothing that greed or envy could win, equals the reward of a spring morning on a lonely Cornish cliff, so quiet that you are truly at one with nature, listening to the sea touching the rocks, sinking one's mind into unplanned beauty.

A miaow. A sharp miaow, almost a yap. Oliver, a couple of yards away from me, turned on his back amid a cluster of celandines, and looked at me from his upside down position.

'Why,' I asked, 'do you think, do many cats think that it is so attractive to be upside down?'

A quiver of the paws.

'All right, I'll tickle you.'

It wasn't, of course, strictly a tickle that was being demanded of me. It was attention. Cats may meander on their individual ways, may haughtily pass by a human who is frantically trying to woo them, may refuse a purr when there seems to be no reason not to purr, yet . . . there are moments when an uncontrollable desire comes over them to be loved. Thereupon they produce one of their endearing tricks, or what their past experience has proved to be endearing . . . they will jump on a lap just when a meal is beginning, or when the owner of the lap has just decided to rise from his seat, or jump on a bed and snuggle up to the occupant at the moment when the occupant is about to get up. The upside down trick is particularly successful out of doors. It is never performed too close to the person for whom it is being played, because the purpose of the trick is to watch its effect. Thus, when cats perform this trick, they do so at a distance of three or four yards from the victim. Upside down they go, wiggle a little, and watch. Oliver watched, and won.

It is, however, unwise to offer a cat too much evidence of his victory because, if you do, he will have a second one. Suddenly, as you are murmuring suitable remarks to him, bent double as you stroke him, he will do a twist and turn and be on his feet and away. One moment seductively appealing, the next, elusive and remote, making you feel a fool. I had no intention of letting Oliver make me feel a fool and so, while he was still blissfully happy on his back, I seized him in my hands and marched him off through a gap between two rows of blackthorn, down a step to the

90

bottom meadow of the cliff and over to a grassy bank of primroses and the scented white flowers of the sea-sandwort. I was proving to him that I was in charge. My one-time anti-cat feelings were always waiting to reassert themselves.

Oliver did not, however, show any signs of resenting my outburst of discipline. Indeed, he was a cat who so rejoiced in the life he had found for himself that he was tolerant of any demands I made on him. Only Ambrose annoyed him sometimes; and then, in an eruption of bad temper, he would have a bash at him with his paw. It was as if, on such occasions, he was thinking: '*You* have no idea of what the struggle of life is about. You have never suffered like me. You have everything given to you without struggling at all.'

SEVEN

Thus Oliver and I sat there in the meadow close to the sea for an hour or more. Oliver, from time to time, would wander off for a while, then come hastening back as if in fear that I might have gone away and left him; and he would greet me with a noisy miaow followed by a purr as he settled himself on my lap. He would purr for several minutes, and then it was time for him to be off again among the primroses, bluebells, the dying daffodil foliage, and time for him to investigate again the mysteries which lay in the undergrowth of the blackthorn. I would watch him go, musing, thinking of the New Year resolution I had begun to fulfil a couple of weeks before, that of reading Marcel Proust again, his *Remembrance of Things Past*.

Proust was not fashionable, as he is today, when I first began to read him; and I would not have known of his existence had it not been for an erudite Egyptian, Georges Cattaui, a Secretary in the Egyptian Embassy who, in eccentric fashion, used to skate round Grosvenor House ice rink reading passages from Proust aloud. Grosvenor House ice rink, during this period, was the gathering place on Sunday afternoons of the prettiest girls in London, young actresses, models, débutantes, and I, along with other young men, used regularly to attend these occasions in hopeful expectation. Thus I would spy a pretty girl gliding round the arena in a skater's mini-skirt, aware that I did not have to devise a formal introduction because all I had to do was to skate in her vicinity, then cunningly, as if by mistake due to the mêlée of the other skaters, bump into her. I had many successful bumps and several friendships as a result.

I was not, however, as confident within myself as my actions would appear. Thus I would make a bump, mutter my apologies, perhaps gain a response from the girl, even find her accepting my invitation to tea on the balcony overlooking the rink, but then, alone with her, I would have nothing to say. My mind would be blank. There I was with the gorgeous result of my bump beside me, and I was tongue-tied.

I was also, at this stage, suffering from the mistaken belief that my whims, my doubts, my desires, my sense of inadequacy, my foolish ambitions, were exclusive to myself, and that no one else suffered in the same way. Then, one Sunday afternoon as I skated round the rink with Georges Cattaui, small and dapper, with an expressive use of his hands, a neat black moustache, a black suit, bursting into French as often as he spoke in English, he pronounced to me that if I were to understand the language of love, or of culture, or of grace and manners in aristocratic places, I must follow his example and become a student of Proust. I do not know if he himself ever learnt much about love, though he was certainly well acquainted with aristocratic places. Like Proust, he was an appalling snob.

It was the wisdom of Proust, however, in which I was interested, just as I was at the time in the wisdom of Somerset Maugham. Maugham was more practical, easier to understand; his stories were related to the present, and they possessed tension. Proust, as I was to learn, had little tension in his chronicles and, unlike Maugham, he demanded of the reader much patience and concentration. Both, on the other hand, shared one quality in common, and that was the gift they gave to a young person, a young person of any period for that matter, of reflecting the emotions of those they wrote about as if in a mirror. A reader looked into the mirror and saw himself.

I have the same volumes of Proust on my shelves as those I bought after Georges Cattaui became my temporary Svengali; and when, the other day, I began reading them again, I was fascinated by the pale pencil marks I had drawn against those passages which had then interested me. They interested me again. The first moment of enlightenment is seldom forgotten.

Here are a few of the passages:

How often is the prospect of future happiness sacrificed to one's impatient insistence upon an immediate gratification.

In this strange phase of love the personality of the woman becomes so enlarged, so deepened that the curiosity which he could now feel aroused in himself, to know the least details in her daily occupation, was the same thirst for knowledge as when he once studied history.

He would at once detect in the story one of those fragments of literal truth which liars, when taken by surprise, console themselves by introducing into the composition of the falsehood which they have to invent, thinking that it will be safely incorporated and will lend the whole story an air of versimilitude.

She failed to see the meaning of his tirade, but she grasped that it was to be included among the scenes of reproach or supplication, scenes which her familiarity with men enabled her to conclude that men would not make unless they were in love: that from the moment they were in love, it was superfluous to obey them, since they would only be more in love later on.

We must confine ourselves to what is possible: no use wasting time in proposing things that cannot be accepted and are declined in advance.

In strange places where our sensations have not been numbed by habit, a girl is remembered and we refresh, we revive an old pain.

Our desires cut across one another's paths, and in this confused existence it is but rarely that a piece of good fortune coincides with the desire that clamoured for it.

A prolonged separation, in soothing rancour, sometimes revives friendship.

With women who do not love us, as with the 'missing', the knowledge that there is no hope left does not prevent our continuing to wait for news.

We tremble when we are in love: but when she has ceased to control our happiness how peaceful, how easy, how bold do we become in her presence.

There can be no peace of mind in love, since the advantage one has secured is never anything but a fresh starting point for further desires.

There are many such passages with the pale pencil marks alongside, and I smile when I look back and remember how important these sagacious remarks were to me at the time. They interpreted the behaviour of a girl towards me, or my behaviour towards her. It was wonderful to have such a secret guide to the peculiar emotions of love. I was now free from the hitherto black and white moods which my solid upbringing had taught me to expect in my relationships with girls. You love her, or you don't love her. You want to sleep with her, or you don't. I was no longer to be held by invisible reins of reason. I now knew that others felt with the same complexity as I sometimes felt. My doubts, conflicts within myself, confidence at one moment, fear of what the girl may be thinking of me making me dumb at the next, were not, as I now learnt, the unique feelings of myself. Proust, at that stage of my life, provided me with the education I required.

I found, however, on re-reading him that he was as

heavy going as ever. Page after page of long, rambling sentences seem to be leading nowhere, and then suddenly you find a flash of enlightenment and your patience is rewarded. He has now, of course, become a fashionable writer among intellectuals and so his work, and himself, are subject to a plethora of treatises, theories, sneers, interpretations, and all the other kinds of self-conscious attention which the famous receive when they are in vogue.

On the other hand, although he may be in vogue, he will never be popular. His world of Dukes, Duchesses, Barons and Parisian Society hostesses is archaic now that 'working class' has become the snob phrase of the age. He is also too introspective for the majority. Union leaders, the prophets of today, are unlikely to urge their members to look inside themselves, instead of inside their pay packets; and the rest of us in our hurrying lives, absorbed by financial self-survival, shy from the discipline which is necessary, preferring to find relaxation by letting our minds go blank and staring vacuously at the television screen, meekly surrendering the opportunities of getting to know ourselves. Instead, we drift with the herd, making ourselves believe that the hysteria of mass decisions, mass emotions, mass pleasures, provide the answer to our lives. Yet it does not require much effort of thought to realise that this is a false belief. Each of us was born with an ego, a soul, or whatever you like to call the sense of Being; each of us is unique, and each of us is a puzzle which we should try to unravel. Otherwise, we are like a man with the key to his own house, who refuses to unlock the door.

It was around the time of my introduction to Proust that I discovered Rabindranath Tagore and his *Sadhana,* the Realisation of Life, and also the Edwin Arnold translations of other Indian philosophers. I still have my original copy of *Sadhana* and it, too, has many passages with pale pencil marks alongside. This careful documentation of my reading suggests I was an earnest young man. Not so. I was a deb's delight at the time and seldom went to bed before

Man must realise the wholeness of his existence, his place in the infinite; he must know that hard as he may strive he can never create his honey within the cells of his hive, for the perennial supply of his life food is outside their walls. He must know that when man shuts himself out from the vitalising and purifying touch of the infinite, and falls back upon himself for his sustenance and his healing, then he goads himself into madness, tears himself into shreds, and eats his own substance. Deprived of the background of the whole, his poverty loses its one great quality which is simplicity, and becomes squalid and shamefaced. His wealth is no longer magnanimous; it grows merely extravagant. His appetites do not minister to his life, keeping to the limits of its purpose; they become an end in themselves and set fire to his life and play the fiddle in the lurid light of the conflagration. Then it is that in our self-expression we try to startle and not to attract; in art we strive for originality and lose sight of truth which is old and yet ever new; in literature we miss the complete view of man which is simple and yet great, but he appears as psychological problem or the embodiment of a passion that is intense because abnormal and because exhibited in the glare of a fiercely emphatic light which is artificial. When man's consciousness is restricted only to the immediate vicinity of his human self, the deeper roots of his nature do not find permanent soil, his spirit is ever on the brink of starvation, and in the place of healthful strength he substitutes stimulation.

A long passage, but read it; and again.

I was endeavouring at this stage of my reading to form a philosophy in which I could believe out of personal conviction, and not because it was imposed upon me. I could not accept, for instance, the value of the notion that all men are equal in the sight of God, when it was so perfectly obvious they varied drastically in their physical and mental attributes. It seemed absurd to me that some-one who was born to permanent ill-health should be considered to have the same chance for a happy life as the man who was capable of breaking the four-minute mile;

and equally absurd to accept the cry of 'fair shares for all' when some are born with much talent, and others with none; when there are some who become great musicians, others who remain tone deaf; some who become skilled in their professions, others who are fit only for manual work; some who are scholars, others who are dunces; some who have the flair to organise, others who can only follow; some who have criminal minds, others with integrity; some who are mean, others who are generous. . . . I could not accept that the multitude of permutations involving the personality of human beings warranted the belief we were all equal; and that we each had one life, and were then wafted to heaven or hell. The prospect did not satisfy me.

It was unfair; and it was ludicrous to expect the unfairness could be corrected by laws, regulations, and political dreams. The unfairness was fundamental, not man-made. Nor had it anything to do with the environment in which one was born, for history had shown the rich could be dunces; the poor could provide a genius.

I also could not accept the way religions competed for converts, as if they were postage stamps for a collection. I was influenced against these methods when I lived in the South Seas and saw, even on small islands, missionaries of various faiths, Protestant, Roman Catholic, Jehovah Witnesses, selling their faiths to the confused and hitherto happy inhabitants as if they were representatives of competing industrial companies. People, I feel, should find their faith without being threatened by a form of spiritual blackmail.

My own faith, and I have no strident zeal about it, no wish to convert anyone, inclines to the doctrine of the transmigration of souls. The doctrine was established and accepted by the Hindus of Buddha's time, the period when Jerusalem was being taken by Nebuchadnezzar, when Nineveh was falling to the Medes, and Marseilles was founded by the Phoenicians. This Indian doctrine long ago helped to persuade me that a human being, in whatever circumstances he has been born and whatever his talents, or lack of them, is judged by the way he conducts himself during his life. If he strives to improve his mind and his talents, he will be promoted, mentally and factually, when he returns to this earth; if he squanders his talents, he will sink lower. Of course, you may scoff at this theory but, to me, this is a religious thought that offers a practical aim for mankind; and it is an explanation of why there are those who are far superior in intellect, or physical achievement to the rest of us. Thus the sick, the unlucky, those who strive without success, those who are selfless in helping others, those who are very poor, those who are stupid, all have a target to aim for. By their conduct in life, in their different lives for that matter, they can still reach perfection. They can become a *rishi*. Who are the *rishis?* Here is Tagore again:

They who having attained the supreme soul in knowledge were filled with wisdom, and having found him in union with the soul were in perfect harmony with the inner self; they having realised him in the heart were free from all selfish desires, and having experienced him in all the activities of the world, had attained calmness. The *rishis* were they who having reached the supreme God from all sides had found abiding peace, had become united with all, had entered into the life of the Universe.

The sweetness of this attainment is that it does not depend upon the conditions in which you live. It is the peace which you can find in your soul which counts; and the soul is your personal possession throughout your journey towards perfection.

Thus I am happier in prayer alone on a Cornish cliff than I am being part of a crowd in a church. For I am unmoved by the mumbo-jumbo of the normal religious services, because they seem to me to reflect an automaton form of worship. The details of the service and the manner of those conducting it seem so contrived that the service makes an artificial impression upon me. It has no meaning.

My heart is not touched, nor is my mind. I am watching a charade.

Religion for me, therefore, is not a question of dutifully attending religious services of one denomination or another. Religion for me is a secret affair, very personal, and requiring no conventional religious umbrella to shelter under. I do not believe I would be a better person if I read from the Koran every day, or conscientiously attended Communion, or fasted, or lit candles and confessed away my conscience. I could still be a heathen in my behaviour to others. I could still have only a façade of goodness. I could still be a bigot. I could still be a man of violence. The evidence of this surrounds us today. Religious fervour does not bring peace of mind; and peace of mind is what man searches for.

There are those who help you forward on your search by their example, and priests of all denominations are naturally among them. They do not require the trappings of a stylised service or a formal habit in order to gain respect, because their influence among people arises from their integrity and selflessness and compassion for humanity. Jeannie has an uncle who is such a person: Canon Martin Andrews, one-time Rector of Stoke Climsland in Cornwall and a Chaplain to the Royal Family. He is not strictly an uncle; he is a cousin but, because he is many years older, she has always called him uncle.

When he retired from Stoke Climsland—the living and the district belong to the Duchy of Cornwall—he went to live at Downderry in a house with a garden edging the cliff, the outline of Looe Island in the distance, and the light of the Eddystone winking at night. He is ninety years old. After the First World War he became a personal friend of the then Prince of Wales and with his encouragement he set up a market garden based on the Rectory in order to help the unemployed and, at one time, employed a hundred men. During the last war he kept open house at the Rectory for Australian airmen. One of these, Peter

Stafford, manager of the Mandarin Hotel in Hong Kong, has never forgotten the peace he found there on his leaves and regularly, once a year, flies back to England to see him. Martin Andrews is that kind of man. Friendship with him is for ever.

Jeannie and I have a hilarious time when we visit him. He has such gusto and perception and dry humour. Jeannie brings an offering of a bone for Honey, his golden labrador, before we have an opulent lunch prepared by Vincent Curtis who has been with Martin since a boy. Vincent used to manage the market garden. Vincent is also known as one of the most imaginative flower arrangers of today. He is a man of many other gifts and he might have made use of them in other spheres, but he is devoted to Martin and, therefore, inevitably he is happy at Downderry.

Recently Martin wrote his autobiography, *Canon's Folly*. A. L. Rowse wrote the Foreword and part of this is worth quoting because it explains why Martin Andrews is one of those who, by their example, help people forward in their search for peace of mind:

Martin Andrews [writes A. L. Rowse] will disapprove of what I am going to say . . . humble man of heart that he is; but I don't care: I have got to say why it is that we all love him, not only here in Cornwall, where he has spent so much of his working life, but everybody who has come in contact or worked with him . . . .

What a happy life it has been, brimming with goodwill, crowded with fascinating incidents and people from the top to the bottom of society, from the Royal Family who have found a friend in him from one generation to another, down to the poor fellows out of work in the 1930s and the soldier to be shot at dawn for desertion at the Front in the horrors of the 1914–1918 war.

The sheer goodness of the man and what he has done for others, in a life lived for others. The humanity of it all, the compassion for men's suffering, the immediate readiness to do something about it, the understanding patience, and good humour. . . .

As A. L. Rowse expected, Martin did disapprove. 'Far too kind, dearie,' he said. 'Not me at all.' He addresses everyone as 'dearie'.

He loves donkeys, and he always wishes to know about Penny and Fred. He once had a donkey called Alphonse at a time when he was a parson in Khartoum; and he used to ride Alphonse around his parish. It was suitable, he said, that a parson should ride such a holy animal; and when one day he was invited to return to England, the only doubt in his mind about accepting was whether he could leave Alphonse. He respected donkeys.

'After all, dearie . . . few animals are mentioned in the Bible more often than the donkey. The infant Christ was saved from Herod by the donkey who carried him safely into Egypt . . . and it was the donkey who carried Christ in triumph to Jerusalem on that first Palm Sunday. No wonder, dearie, that all donkeys have the Cross on their backs.'

It so happened that, shortly after this particular visit to Martin, we were informed that the new Bishop of Truro, the Rt Reverend John Leonard, intended to pay us a 'visitation'. The prospect of such a 'visitation' mildly alarmed us, as we had no experience of Bishops except at long ago Confirmation time when, I remember, I was petrified. I was the last in a long line of boys in Harrow School Chapel who had to advance up the aisle to the then Bishop of London. No reason at all for such nerves, except shyness.

The Bishop, we were warned, would be on a rush tour of the district and would be with us at half past two and stay for a quarter of an hour. I ruminated what I might say to him, but decided against telling him that, although I felt at peace in the sanctity of an empty church, I was not so at peace in a full one. On the other hand, I was tempted to put before him a suggestion about paying for the upkeep of churches but, again, decided to say nothing because no note of controversy should be introduced in such a short 'visitation'. The suggestion I had in mind was that local people should be invited to pay an annual subscription just for the pleasure of *looking* at their local church. After all a church, whether you are a churchgoer or not, gives comfort and represents to the eye of the beholder centuries of prayer. When, however, I once proposed this idea to a vicar I was put in my place. 'We want you in the church,' was the gist of his reply. 'We don't want you paying for the privilege of not coming.'

At twenty-five minutes past two on the appointed day I stationed myself on the bridge, just as on that night I had waited for George Brown, and stood so that I could see a car coming down the lane and see it turn a hundred yards on from Monty's Leap, thus giving me time to alert Jeannie that the 'visitation' was about to begin.

We had already discussed what we should offer the Bishop when he arrived; something which could be consumed within a quarter of an hour. Obviously he would have had lunch. Equally obviously it was too soon to offer him a Cornish cream tea. Thus we decided upon coffee and brandy; and in readiness Jeannie cleaned the silver and I, in my Martha capacity, cleaned the house.

'A Land Rover is coming down the lane!' I called out to Jeannie from the bridge.

I had expected a more formal vehicle.

'It's the Vicar's Land Rover!'

The Vicar's Land Rover resembled a farmer's second-hand Land Rover; well used, blurred paint and functional. The Vicar himself, John Friggens, is a charming person and much respected in St Buryan, whose inhabitants are half Protestant and half Methodist.

I hastened back to join Jeannie, then went to the window to peer at the Land Rover's arrival. It pulled to a stop outside the barn and, a moment later, out stepped the Vicar, his curate, and the Bishop. Thereupon Jeannie and I raced round to the front to greet them.

'Welcome, my lord,' I said, and felt very unnatural in

doing so, but had been told that this was how one first addressed a Bishop, and that thereafter it was 'sir'.

He looked resplendent. He wore a cerise robe with a gold Cross on a chain hanging from his neck; jewelled rings were on his fingers, and in his right hand he was holding, as if it were a walking stick, a tall crook. He was bareheaded, dark, of medium height and good looking and my first impression, with all due respect to my fellow Cornishmen, was to wonder why such an urbane cleric should have chosen to come to Cornwall.

'It is very nice of you to visit us,' said Jeannie, politely.

'Ah,' said the Bishop, looking around and gazing across the moorland to the sea, 'this is the kind of place where I would like to live.'

A remark which immediately endeared him to us.

We proceeded to walk up the path, and had turned the corner of the cottage to go into the porch when, from the donkeys' favourite watching point in the field above the small garden, came an enormous bellow.

Fred had seen the Bishop.

We could not hear ourselves speak. It was a bellow, up and down the scale in ever-increasing crescendo, as if trumpeters of the Brigade of Guards were hailing the Queen. It was the bellow which Fred reserves for the most special occasions, such as when the *QE2* visited Minack. It was Fred at his most excited. A Bishop! A Bishop has come to see me!

The Bishop was enchanted.

'A donkey!'

'Fred,' I said, 'and that's Penny behind him.' Poor Penny, with her strangled cry of a hee-haw, could not compete with her son.

'I must speak to him,' said the Bishop, charmingly, catching Fred's mood.

'If you'll follow me.'

I led the way past the fuchsia bush with its flowers hanging like miniature red Chinese lanterns, and across the small patch of ground to the wrought-iron gate through which the donkeys come in and out of the big field.

'Come on, Fred!' I called out. 'Come and meet the Bishop.'

The Bishop leaned his crook against the wall and bent over the gate, his gold Cross and chain dangling.

'Come on, Fred!' I called out again.

Suddenly the bellow died away, first to a sound like a flute, then to a whisper, then to silence. Total silence.

Fred had come to the gate and had turned his bottom to the Bishop. The dark brown lines along his spine and down each shoulder were clearly to be seen.

'Look, Bishop,' he seemed to be saying, 'I've got a Cross too.'

EIGHT

The sun was on the lintel, the massive rough granite lintel above the fireplace. It was no splash of sun. It was a shaft, the size of a fist.

'Summer has begun,' I said to Jeannie, who was in the kitchen preparing dinner.

The sun had moved far enough west for it to be setting below the hill of the donkey field; and as it dipped there came a moment when it filtered through the glass of the porch, through the open doorway, and touched the old stone. Each evening, each week, it moved across the lintel until high summer was over; and then back it would come, imperceptibly moving to the point where we had first seen it, and then it would vanish. Autumn, winter, spring would pass before we saw it again.

'A warning,' said Jeannie from the kitchen.

'How do you mean, a warning?'

The tiny kitchen is part of the sitting-room, although it is cunningly hidden; and you would not know it was there unless you looked round the corner over the stable-type door. It was over this door that Jeannie's face appeared. She was laughing.

'A warning,' she said, 'that the year is going by and the New Year resolutions are not being achieved.'

'That's not true.'

'Nearly six months of the year,' she said, 'and you haven't yet fried a sausage.'

'That was never a resolution.'

'Just a joke. I was thinking of the gourmet's dinner you promised; the exquisite cuisine I was going to enjoy after sitting back and watching you prepare it.'

'There was the onion soup.'

'Delicious, the best I've ever tasted, and such skill on your part and patience. . . .'

'You're joking again.'

'No, seriously . . . I *am* looking forward to that dinner.'

'Don't worry, you'll have it. There's plenty of time.' Then, I added: 'I've done well with the seeds anyhow. That's one resolution fulfilled!'

Rows of seedboxes, like soldiers on parade, lined the path below the rose garden. Some empty, the seedlings having already been planted out, most of them full. Four full boxes of Snowdrift alyssum, three of Rosie O'Day, a deep rose pink alyssum; four boxes of Blue Blazer ageratum; five boxes of Suttons Triumph antirrhinum, first introduced to flower growers in 1935; two boxes of balsam; four boxes of Sunshine Calceolaria Rugosa, catalogued as one of the most expensive flower seeds in the world, and promising to be a brilliant yellow and weather resisting; two boxes of cosmea, described as having fine, fern-like foliage and lovely tall flowers like single dahlias; a box of sunflowers; eight boxes of lobelia, Cambridge Blue and dark blue Crystal Palace; four boxes of nicotiana, the fragrant tobacco plant; seven boxes of Majestic Giant mixed pansies; four boxes of rudbeckia, late flowering and resembling huge coloured daisies; two boxes of salvia; and two of zinnia.

This sumptuous array of small plants fascinated me, fascinated me, in fact, so much that Jeannie used to explain to visitors who admired them that they were going to be there for ever. 'He doesn't seem to be thinking of the garden,' she would say. 'He just wants to keep them in the boxes and look at them.'

New growers of their own plants will understand how I felt. Always before I had collected boxes of plants from someone else who had done the work and it had been as easy, as impersonal, as buying goods at a supermarket. Now, at last, after the years of being a commercial grower of potatoes, daffodils, tomatoes and flowers of all sorts, I had grown plants for my own pleasure. Moreover, I reckoned that the total number of plants were worth nearly £50 against the cost of around £5 for seed and £5 for commercially prepared composts. Pride in achievement, therefore, was coupled with satisfaction in my economy; and so those who have experienced this small delight, will understand why I went on looking at the plants, watching them growing larger and larger in their boxes, rather than transplanting them into the rough world of the garden where I could not cosset them so easily against drying out, against slugs and snails, or against the wind.

I owed much to Percy Potter, who is in charge of the Sutton Trial Grounds at Gulval near Penzance, and to William Hocking, his assistant, for preliminary advice. They are born gardeners, growing by instinct and an inherent experience; and Percy speaks a Fred Streeter language.

'Look at them tractors,' Percy said to me the other day. 'Pounding the soil into concrete. How do they expect to get a decent crop? Then soon after they've planted whatever it is the tractors will be over the ground again spraying . . . killing the insects, killing the weeds. It's all very well, but were we ever intended to treat nature like this? My old man used to say that gentle steel manuring was the finest thing you could do to a crop in a field or a garden. Steel manuring, you know what I mean, a steady shifting of the soil with a hoe.'

He has his failures, seeds which mysteriously fail to germinate; and the year of my seedboxes gave me a chance to joke at him.

'Can I help you out, Percy?'

Or:

'Your alyssum isn't doing well . . . I've plenty to spare. You're welcome to some!'

And Percy would turn to Jeannie:

'Great gardener he thinks he is . . . I might as well go home and he can take over!'

'The snag is, Percy,' Jeannie said laughing, 'he doesn't know what is in his seedboxes.'

'Rubbish, Jeannie.'

She was, however, partly correct. I had failed to buy an indelible pencil and, after sowing the seeds, I had used an ordinary pen to write on each label. As a result of my stupid act, the ink inevitably faded away until, too late, I discovered that the writing on each label had become an indecipherable smudge. Thus Rosie O'Day could have been Snowdrift; Sunshine Calceolaria Rugosa could have been balsam; nicotiana could have been rudbeckia; Crystal Palace lobelia could have been Blue Blazer ageratum. Yet, confusing as this may have been, the little plants looked splendid; and I was proud of the way I had both sown them and transplanted them, first in seed compost, then in potting compost. The fact I didn't know what they were was incidental.

I had had my difficulties in growing them. The seed-boxes had first been placed on the bench in the small green-house where we bunch daffodils and, as seed growing and daffodil bunching for a while coincided, the boxes were placed at one end close to the lemon tree. This position, perhaps because of the sweet smelling leaves of the lemon tree, was also much favoured by Oliver, and the presence of the seedboxes did not alter his wish to lie there. Hence I would come into the greenhouse and find him comfortably curled up on the Cambridge Blue lobelia and I would proceed to remove him. I think he was puzzled by my behaviour, for I showed no hasty irritation, no shouting at him . . . I just gently picked him up and took him out.

The reason for my gentleness is easy to guess. Had I scared him, he would have churned up the seedbox compost in the manner of a dirt track rider.

I solved this problem in due course by laying wire netting over the seedboxes; and later, after the seedlings were transplanted, the potted boxes were placed in the larger greenhouse and the door kept shut. It was not until I first began to plant them in the garden that trouble began again. Ambrose joined Oliver in causing the trouble.

Ambrose's distrust of the human race had appeared to be diminishing now that summer had come. Perhaps the sun lulled him. Perhaps the young rabbits he caught fed him into being such a satisfied cat that he was too lazy to be temperamental. True, he went into a panic if a stranger approached him, and he continued to refuse to be picked up or to jump on my lap . . . but there were subtle signs that his character was changing. For instance, he would come for walks with us and Oliver, and occasionally on these walks he would stop close in front of me, look up with a beatific Pollyanna face, and wait for me to stroke him. There I would be on a path, waist high bracken on either side, foxgloves peering their purple spires towards the sky, young green brambles scraping my legs as I walked, and down below me would be Ambrose, hinting that he was prepared to show me affection. Inevitably I felt flattered. Inevitably I stooped, and responded.

These walks, however, had their hazards. One of them took us up the lane across Monty's Leap and on round the bend where we turned right up a grassy path through moorland. When we reached the top, we turned right again with a bramble hedge on our left and a stone hedge spattered with blackthorn bushes on our right. Then on through bracken land and past a large badger sett, the same sett where the beagle was caught in a snare, and then right again down a sloping path towards the sea and the Coastal Path. The Coastal Path led back to Minack land and up the hill of Fred's field, where at the top we left it and passed through the white gate leading home to the cottage. The walk, even if we took it at a meandering pace, did not last more than twenty minutes, and we always set off in the early morning before there was any threat of strangers walking the Coastal Path.

The Coastal Path is, of course, an admirable institution, and the long stretch from Mousehole around Land's End to St Ives is one of the most beautiful walks in the world. It was completed in 1973 but, before that, we always kept our own section open to the public with direction signs, apart from clearing the undergrowth at those times of the year when it was in danger of hiding the path. It is a walk for the solitary, those who can gain more from the steep climbs, from the rugged beauty of sea-lashed rocks and pocket meadows, than the mere pleasure of exercise. Most of the walkers realise this, but the path also attracts the urban hikers who walk in packs, heads down, their belongings heaped on their backs so that they remind one of snails; and they pause only when they have their sandwiches and cakes, scattering paper and empty beer cans as a memorial of their passing. There are, too, the vandals. The Cornwall County Council erected wooden direction signs instead of the crude and ugly metal ones which are usually used for footpaths; and because they are of wood they can be smashed, and thus many *have* been smashed. Such walkers, however, are in the minority, and only occasionally do I find debris on Minack land; and this is perhaps helped by a typewritten notice I put on a board where the Coastal Path begins on Minack land. The notice read: YOU ARE VERY WELCOME TO CROSS THIS PRIVATE PROPERTY ALONG THE PATH WHICH IS MARKED.

The other day I had a look at this notice, and scrawled across it were the words: You own nothing . . . it belongs to *us*.

One morning this early summer Jeannie and I, Oliver and Ambrose, set off on the round walk, as we call it, soon after breakfast, and had reached the point when we were walking downhill towards the sea and the Coastal Path, when I spied coming towards us but away on the path in Fred's field, a man and a woman, a child and a dog. At that moment they were in the distance, a mass of bracken, blackthorn and a couple of stone hedges in between . . . but I realised that if they continued on their route, an unleashed dog along with them, we would meet head on when we arrived at the Coastal Path. Such a meeting would scatter Oliver and Ambrose; and so I sang out across the narrow valley:

'Would you mind putting your dog on the lead?'

There was no response, and I called out again.

Still no response, but I saw them stop, have a word with each other, the woman hatless, the man in a peaked cap like that of a French fisherman; and then I heard the shout of his reply:

'Mind your own business!'

This was unexpected.

'I've two cats here,' I yelled back, 'and I don't want the dog to chase them!'

This was ridiculous. A lovely morning, two peaceful cats, and here was I having a shouting argument on their behalf across the valley.

'Cats!' I shouted, hands cupped to mouth. 'Two cats!'

An epithet came hurtling back in reply.

At this instant, the woman leashed the dog, but the man, a tug at his cap, began to stride purposefully towards us.

'We had better turn back,' said Jeannie.

'Fine,' I said, 'if the cats do likewise.'

'Oliver . . . Ambrose,' Jeannie beseeched.

Thereupon Oliver bolted forwards, and Ambrose bolted backwards.

'Now we've done it,' I said.

'Oliver! Ambrose!'

Both, but in opposite directions, had disappeared into the bracken.

'We must be sensible,' I said.

'That means you'll have to go forward to look for Oliver, and I'll go backwards to look for Ambrose.'

'The man!' I replied.

He had now jumped over our boundary hedge and was striding along the Coastal Path looking like a football fan on the rampage. The peaked cap gave him an arrogant, threatening air.

'Oliver! . . . Oliver!'

As I called, I walked on towards the Coastal Path and, just as I reached it, out of the undergrowth on my right dashed Oliver. He ran back towards Jeannie, and I faced the gentleman alone.

'Thank you,' I said to him, when he came within speaking distance, recalling the woman leashing the dog. 'Thank you for holding your dog.'

I was hoping my face displayed a friendly smile. I can never be sure how my face looks. I have passed people, believing I was smiling at them, and Jeannie has said: 'Why did you look so glum?'

We were now within a few yards of each other.

'I'm sure,' I said to him—he wore a trim black beard and this, with his French fisherman's cap, reminded me of a character in a Simenon story—'I'm sure you will understand when I tell you that I was trying to protect my cats.'

'Bloody hell I do,' he replied in unmistakable English.

Reluctantly I felt my adrenalin rising.

Foxgloves galore around us, the first bursting of elderberry flower saucers, fragment of a white sail of a yacht seen through the branches of a blackthorn, swifts diving over Fred's field, a magpie coarsely cackling, all the wild, natural extravagance of nature, scents of the sea roaming from the rocks, glint of the sun on pink campion, an early honeysuckle, rich golden gorse, arenas of white stitchwort . . . and all at the innocent beginning of a day.

'I *do* want to explain,' I said and, as I spoke, I was

growing more angry every second. 'You see, they are two very nervous cats, and they don't expect to meet anyone on this walk, and if they meet a dog. . . .'

'A dog has as much right to be here as any damned cat.'

'Rights'. . . the most disturbing, contemporary word in the British language. The right to strike, the right to have a wage rise, the right to do this, or do that, the right to be equal without any effort to earn such equality . . . an arid word because it brings no satisfaction. One 'right' achieved only breeds another.

'Of course, dear fellow,' I said, controlling my rising adrenalin by adopting a patronising tone. 'Nobody is contesting the right of your dog to be here . . . it's just that I didn't think you would want it to chase my cats.'

He glared at me. No peacemaking on his part.

'Anyhow,' I went on, 'you are obviously a stranger around here. On beautiful mornings in this area people who love it do not lose their temper.'

I turned my back on him and returned up the path to Jeannie.

'Oliver is here,' she said, and there was Oliver crouching a yard away, 'but no sign of Ambrose.'

There was no sign of Ambrose for the rest of the morning; for the rest of the afternoon as well, in fact. We called and we called. The innocent morning walk had turned into one of strain and distress. A sea of green bracken and in it, somewhere, was Ambrose, listening to our anguished cries, amused by them, saying to himself that he would extract the maximum pleasure from them before he reappeared. It was, however greed which retrieved him in the end. Jeannie cooked some fish and, while it was still hot and the aroma strong, she carried the saucepan at bracken height along the path. A clever move. Ambrose could not resist it.

Nor, unfortunately, could he resist my plants when I

began to set them out in the garden. Nor could Oliver. They stalked around like sinister members of the Mafia, watching me as I grouped the little plants in various corners, waiting for me to turn my back, waiting to pounce on a plant, then treating it as a football, deftly digging it up with a paw and tossing it from one to another.

'Stop it!' I would shriek when I saw them and they would scurry away into the safety of the escallonia, the massive bush of felt-like green leaves and clusters of pink flowers opposite the path to the porch, which we call Escallonia Towers; and they would sit there, heads peeping among the leaves, unashamedly prepared to play football again as soon as the opportunity occurred.

Jeannie thought them funny.

'They're only trying to be a Georgie Best,' she said.

'And look what happened to him,' I replied.

'Oh, just watch them now!'

I watched, and saw an ageratum sailing into the air.

'Damn you . . . get away, get away!'

And this time they raced down the path, side by side, coming to a stop close to the wooden gate of the small yard in front of the barn where the donkeys were peering over the fence, observing the scene.

Of course, I was not as angry as I appeared to be. My emotions are stronger than my deeds, and the loss of my temper has never been of much significance. I understand, however, why cats sometimes enrage people. When I was a cat hater I was often enraged; and I recall a period when I lived in Manchester in Portsmouth Street, off Ackers Street then famed for its theatrical digs, and I was maddened by the caterwauling of cats in the neighbourhood of my bedroom window. Night after night I was kept awake by their noise, and I used to lie in my bed plotting methods for their destruction. The method I decided upon was the use of a water pistol.

I had been given this tip about a water pistol when I

was a child at Glendorgal, which was then our family home near Newquay, and it was given me by the old gardener. A seedbed of his had recently been punctured by the activities of strange cats and he was telling me how he succeeded in stopping their vandalism.

'I kept a water pistol at the ready,' he explained, 'and I lay in wait for a cat and when I saw it coming over the hedge and across the garden towards this lovely seedbed of newly sown carrots, broccoli and lettuce, I aimed the water pistol at it, pressed the trigger . . . and away ran the cat. Cats don't like water, you know.'

The old gardener had no wish to harm his enemy. His object was to frighten him. He was not like a well-known comedian to whom I listened on a radio programme. He declared he shot up cats with an air gun when they came into his garden. He justified this cruelty on the grounds that he was protecting the birds in his garden and, of course, no one can deny that cats catch birds, although I know of many exceptions. Monty and Lama were exceptions, so also are Oliver and Ambrose. True, I have known Ambrose catch a dunnock, but a dunnock hopping on the ground resembles a mouse and so perhaps there is an excuse for Ambrose's action. I was on the same radio programme myself a little while later and, remembering the comedian's outburst, I set out the point of view that the catching of birds by cats was part of the cycle of nature. Hawks kill birds, magpies, jackdaws, carrion crows steal nestlings, foxes catch gulls . . . and so perhaps the distress of seeing a cat catch a bird can be eased by putting its act in this perspective.

I did not, as it happens, use a water pistol to scatter my Manchester caterwauling cats. Each morning when I awoke the annoyance they had caused me seemed unimportant. The midnight wake often ends in this way. The angry letter composed in the darkness is never written. The determination to follow a certain course is unfulfilled. Fine plans become muted. Cool sense dissipates wild ideas. Even unhappiness can be dispelled. The thoughts of a midnight wake are usually deceptive.

Cats, I have now learnt since my cat-hater times, offer subtleties of pleasure that earn them forgiveness for their irritations. They have grace and style and a sweetness of movement, a detached elegance, and a marvellous devotion to those they choose to love. Cats are not for the coarse. I cannot vision a militant besotted by his rights having the time to appreciate a cat. A cat would be far too subtle for him. A cat, in my young days, was too subtle for me.

Now, however, my edgy moments can be soothed by watching Oliver, without a care in the world, strolling up the lane from Monty's Leap, pausing at the sound of a rustle in the grass, investigating, then meandering onwards; and, when the news bulletins bellow their stories of envy and dissatisfaction I can find consolation in observing Ambrose spreading himself in abandonment under the syringa bush, just as Monty used to do under the syringa bush at Mortlake. Thus I am now educated to forgive them their antics. I forgive them for using an ageratum as a football, or for digging up my bed of mignonette, that old fashioned flower, the seeds of which are so loth to germinate, or for removing with a flurry of paws my patch of night-scented stock that has just broken green from the soil close to the porch door.

These are the hazards that gardeners must expect if they have cats around the house. Thus my loss of temper, my shouting at them, were mock gestures of annoyance. I had learnt to tolerate them in the garden. I was satisfied with the compensations I received. There was, however, one bastion which they had failed to conquer, and that was the bed. True to my resolution, I still kept them at bay. I would come into the bedroom from my bath and find Oliver curled on the eiderdown; and I would ruthlessly pick him up and carry him to the porch and deposit him on the cane chair. I was adamant that I should not spend my nights cramped and immobile; and if Oliver were allowed to

119

remain, would not Ambrose be soon to follow? And yet . . . each time I removed Oliver, I seemed to be doing so more gently.

Once again I found myself questioning my attitude towards animals; towards all creatures of nature. Was it, in fact, an indulgence on my part? Love, kindness, understanding, being a reflection of my mood at the time? And if I were not in that mood, if it did not suit me, did I not change my attitude?

The snails are a case in point. At the first shower of spring, the snails emerged from their hibernation hideouts, trailed their slimy marks over the rocks, the soil, and immediately small pansies disappeared, French marigolds became stumps and tobacco plants had large bites in their leaves. Snails are the murderers of a young garden; yet I am fascinated by their innate determination for survival and how they exist throughout the growing year despite the ceaseless attack on them by thrushes and blackbirds and humans. Thus, in an effort to preserve both them and the garden, I gathered the snails that were attacking my plants into a bucket and carried the bucket across the stable field, the stable field in front of the barn where the donkeys spend much of their time, and deposited the snails at the bottom of the far hedge.

I felt the better for doing so. I had removed the snails without hurting them. I had proved my affection for the living creatures of nature. I was, if I were to speak the truth, rather proud of myself that I had withstood the temptation of using a proprietary brand of slug and snail bait. I had given the snails a chance to eat elsewhere, nibble weeds instead of plants, enjoy a life away from any angry gardener.

The snails, unfortunately, did not appreciate my good intentions. Jeannie, a day later, was standing in the stable field grooming Penny, when she noticed a concourse of snails around her feet.

'The snails are on their way back to you!' she called out, laughing.

It was funny in one way; sad in another. They did indeed seem to be on their way back, relations included, and any other snails who had heard the news about the man who put snails in a bucket when they annoyed him, then carried them away to live another day. This time, however, I was not so kind.

Each morning I saw the result of their munching, bare leaves, desiccated pansies, and my impatience grew. My mood became no longer one of loving all creatures of nature; my own personal activities were being affected; I was no longer a do-gooder observer; I was involved with the survival of my plants, and so my benevolent attitude changed. My plants were more precious to me than snails and so bait, I decided, had to be used to kill them.

I used a spray. Pellets, unless they are covered, are a menace. Birds pick them up believing they are edible, and dogs and cats eat them, believing they are broken biscuits. Just a few of the pellets being eaten will kill. As for the spray, there is one basic rule. Get up early the next morning after it has been used, and destroy the doped snails before the thrushes and blackbirds pounce upon them.

Thus my sentimental attitude towards snails was shown to be a vacuous one as soon as my interests were at stake . . . so many causes are pursued by people unaffected by the disadvantages of the causes they espouse.

It is the wind, however, not snails, which is the real enemy of the garden, and the salt which comes with it. It sears in from Mount's Bay, white waves wildly flinging foam at each other, crashing against the rocks and the cliff, sending a cloud of salt up into the sky. A sticky mist in the wind, killing the leaves of the elders and the blackthorn, biting into the corners of the garden, finding gaps between bushes, and rushing to where the vegetables are growing, bruising the foot-high runner beans and peas,

121

bashing the raspberry canes . . . spring winds are the killers. For two years in succession they have scythed into Minack so that the elms along the lane have been bared, and the leafless blackthorn and elders have failed in many places to survive. The wind is always our enemy. Only the evergreen leaves of the escallonia are safe against it. They withstand the wind, accept the sticky salt, and remain green.

Cats are not omnipotent.

One night in early June, a night when such a wind was blasting the cottage, I felt a lump at the bottom of the bed; and I put out a hand and touched fur. Oliver, I said to myself, and prepared to get out of bed. Then I felt a second lump. The two of them were there. What should I do? I was sleepy. I was averse to disturbing myself. The noise of the gale lulled my intended determination to be free. Let them be, I dopily said to myself.

And I did.

The first night that Oliver and Ambrose slept on our bed.

A broken New Year's resolution which now brings cramp, night after night, to my legs.

NINE

Broadbent was on the roof. It was raining. It was raining so hard that the noise of it sounded as if pebbles were spraying the porch glass. A fortnight of fine weather had broken; and Broadbent was up there, a bunch of black feathers, squatting close to the apex of the roof, as if the sun were still shining.

'Silly jackdaw,' said Jeannie, looking up at him from the porch.

He was a timid jackdaw. He was not one of those jackdaws which, once they have accepted the attention of a human being, demand so much that they become tyrants. Nor could I boast, in the way that human beings like to boast when a wild animal or bird shows interest in them, that he was tame. He was attached to us because he no doubt instinctively remembered how we had nursed him back to health. We were friendly. We threw him scraps. We were useful, but he did not belong to us.

'This weather makes it a good day for Labour Warms,' I said.

Labour Warms, the massive teak cupboard once in my nursery, containing an accumulation of letters and notebooks over the years, and still displaying in blue letters across its top the exhortation: LABOUR WARMS SLOTH HARMS.

'I can spend the day,' I went on, 'with papers littering the floor.'

'And at the end of it, you'll be able to say that a resolution has been fulfilled,' smiled Jeannie.

'At least I'm proving that I am *trying* to fulfil my resolutions.'

'Very praiseworthy.'

'You're in a sceptical mood again.'

'Oh no, not really. I was just thinking. . . .'

'*What* are you thinking?'

Oliver was sitting on the carpet in front of the bookcase, his twig of a tail curled round him, the tip tapping his front paws.

'I was just thinking how Oliver and Ambrose have triumphed.'

'You were always on their side. You're rubbing it in.'

'It *is* funny, isn't it? That fine New Year resolution to keep them off the bed, and they conquered you. Two cats filling the bed!'

'An act of God.'

Jeannie was laughing.

'Anyhow,' she said, 'sensible of you to be philosophical about it.'

'I'm just being a good loser.'

'Did you hear that, Oliver?' said Jeannie, still laughing. 'He accepts his defeat like a good loser.'

'Enough of this,' I said.

'I'm only teasing you.'

'Oh, I know that . . . but I think it is time to change the subject.'

'To the subject of Labour Warms?'

'Yes.'

'It should be interesting.'

'There's so much. I can only make a start.'

'You'll become full of nostalgia.'

'I'll enjoy that.'

'Some people disapprove of nostalgia. They class it as sentimental indulgence.'

'Do you understand that? I don't. I can never understand the theory that you should always look forward and never look back.'

'Nor do I.'

People who don't want to look back must have led such disturbing lives that they haven't anything they wish to remember. Thus they cling to the future as if it were a lifebelt. They feel safe in the future because it hasn't happened.

I was standing by my Regency kidney-shaped desk filling my pipe; and Jeannie was sitting on the side of the armchair, and Oliver had just jumped on her lap.

'I met a well-meaning social worker the other day,' Jeannie said, 'who told me she was a visitor to an old people's home, and that she had recently scored a great success in her work.'

'What was that?'

'She said that when she first went to the home all the inmates were docile, sat in their chairs dreaming of the past. Her great success was that she changed all that. She said that she had been able to wake them up to the problems that faced us all today, and that they were no longer sitting there remembering. Then she added, excitedly, "do you know what? I have got them arguing with each other, and having rows. I have made them come alive!" '

'I suppose your friend had a point.'

'Oh, rubbish,' said Jeannie. 'Surely arguments on present day problems are no substitute for the quiet those old people were having with their memories?'

'Psychiatrists would probably not agree.'

'Oh, psychiatrists. . . .'

My pipe was filled; filled with tobacco which comes from H. Simmons, the old established tobacconists in Burlington Arcade off Piccadilly, and called Down the

Road, but when I tried to light it the matchstick snapped as soon as it struck the side of the box.

'Damn these matches.'

'I'll buy you a lighter.'

'Lovely . . . next Christmas then.'

There was a knock on the door, and the cry: 'Post!' and Oliver leapt from Jeannie's lap.

A couple of letters, a bill, and a cunningly phrased circular announcing that I had been given a lucky number in a draw for fabulous prizes, provided I bought an album of records.

'I'll go off now,' I said.

'I'll bring you a cup of coffee later on.'

I am one of those who finds it difficult to separate the past from the present. Time, to me, is a plateau. There is no mountain range which hides from me the emotions I once felt; and when, to my joy, I meet again someone whom I knew long ago there is for me no interval between the parting and the reunion. Such an attitude can cause awkward moments. I am brimful of happy memories, but the mind of the other is blank. Or I anticipate a meeting with a friend of my youth, the youthful face still fresh in my thoughts and then, on seeing him, I am startled into remembering a sentence by Leopardi . . . 'seeing again after some years a person I have known young, always at first I seem to see one who has suffered a great calamity.'

I had no clear recall, however, of those who featured on the first piece of paper I extracted from Labour Warms; and for good reason. No one would wish to remember the faces behind the initials of the following school report. I was fourteen and at Harrow.

Latin: Has improved slightly.   R.W.F.

French: Weak, could do better. A nice boy but a bit idle. E.D.L.

English: Poor. I am of the opinion he could try a great deal more if he exerted himself.   R.W.F.

Mathematics: Not very satisfactory—a hindrance to the progress of others. There is no vice—only childish exuberance out of place and time.   J.H.H.

House Master's Report: A very nice interesting boy but really lazy. I have had him on reports, if this does not make him work and stop playing the fool in class sterner methods must be used. I like him very much and I have no doubt he will alter his ways. He is a keen little cricketer.   B.M.

A couple of years later the keen little cricketer won a place in the House cricket eleven but, playing in a vital match, he dropped a catch. That evening B.M., my house-master, summoned me to his study.

'Tangye,' he said, censoriously, 'you're useless to society.'

I had no qualifications when I left Harrow. I had failed to pass any of the appropriate examinations and so I was not viewed upon by prospective employers as being employable. This, of course, has been a perennial problem for school-leavers. If they cannot shove in front of employers paper evidence of their scholastic achievements, they are passed by in favour of those who can. Intelligence, flair (a quality which has no place in any examination, but with a potential more exciting than any), enthusiasm . . . all these are indefinable virtues and valueless without certificates of examination passes. Thus it is that the imaginative young, especially those who are timid, are passed over by those who sail into an examination room without the inhibitions of the imaginative; and so pass, and win favour.

I was lucky. I lived in a period when it was possible to move into a job through a backdoor; and, using the influence of a friend of my father, I was enrolled as a clerk in Unilever. Once there, however, I again became controlled by examination standards and was informed, in due course, that as I possessed no certificates to prove my worth I had little hope of an executive future. This did not worry me. I had already come to the conclusion that, though happy in the company of my colleagues, I was not going to spend the rest of my life selling soap and margarine; and then came my second opportunity to pass through a backdoor. A friend of a girlfriend knew Max Aitken, Beaverbrook's son, and I was given an introduction. Half an hour after the interview began, a dream came true. I was given a month's trial on the *Daily Express* in Manchester.

Had it not been for that introduction, much of what I found in Labour Warms would not have been there. For, as the result of that interview, as the result of my joining the *Daily Express*, I was introduced into a world which would forever have been denied me had I devoted my life to soap and margarine. There is no method in choosing the items I am going to quote; no time sequence. I am just picking out odds and ends from Labour Warms . . . and, in my mind's eye, I see the small boy who looked apprehensively up at the great teak cupboard standing in his nursery.

There is Jeannie's verse about Suez. I remember the horror when, lying in bed with Monty at the bottom of it, I switched on the portable radio to the early morning news and heard that British paratroops had dropped on Egypt and that fighting was in full swing. I was appalled. The attack, at a time when the British Empire was petering into extinction, thanks largely to the attitude of boredom towards such an empire by the British public, seemed to me to be senseless. It was even embarrassing. After all, in comparison with the Soviet Union and the United States, the power Britain possessed was the equivalent of peanuts.

'Oh God,' I said to Jeannie, 'the whole thing is doomed to failure. *How* could it have been started?'

I am not sure when I began to have second thoughts, second thoughts not about the wisdom of the attack but about the reasons which prompted it. The reasons had not been created by the British and the French, I realised.

The reasons had been provided by the American Secretary of State, John Foster Dulles. Dulles had refused to supply President Nasser with arms (as a gesture towards Israel) and Nasser turned to the Russians for his tanks and aircraft. In pique at the deal, Dulles cut off American financial backing for the High Dam at Aswan, a key part of Nasser's plan to bring irrigation to the desert and, in revenge, Nasser nationalised the Suez Canal; and then the British and French were alerted to the likelihood of the Russians usurping their influence in the Middle East and beyond. The Autherine Lucey in Jeannie's verse is the coloured teacher who, at the time, was being banned from teaching in a white American school:

> The foreign policy of Mr Dulles
> Only sullies
> Anglo-American relations.
> And Eisenhower
> Is sour
> And votes against us at United Nations.
> And I would like to do something juicy
> And shout
> What about
> Autherine Lucey?
> And anyway it all began
> With the Aswan Dam.

A pithy verse, appropriate to the mood at the time; and it won the approval of the legendary A. P. Herbert, wit and a mainstay of *Punch* for many years; instigator of the first major Divorce Reform Bill when he was the Independent Member for Oxford University, dramatist, author of musical comedies like *Bless The Bride* (with the glorious music of Vivian Ellis), authority on the stars whose names he wished to change into those of history's heroes, a frustrated follower of and writer about football pools (creator of the Curate's Perm, the Organist's Perm, the Wealthy Widow's Perm), a tenacious pursuer of lost causes, a wonderful companion, and one of the dozen or so honoured in Churchill's resignation list after the war, when he became Sir Alan (much to his surprise).

He often stayed with us at Minack and, one day, he wrote:

> Here come the storm-tossed and the tired
> And find balm for every bane;
> Body and soul refreshed and fired,
> They sadly put to sea again.

The verse is not one of his better ones. I prefer the lines he wrote about two young sisters, Anne and Mary, whom he met one day when he was with us. He wrote it in the family visiting book after a few seconds' pause:

> Be wary man
> Man be wary
> First of Anne
> And then of Mary.

Once we arranged to meet him in Plymouth, staying in the same hotel; and the occasion was a party for a consortium, of which he was a member, that sought the ITV franchise for the South West. The consortium failed to win it, but the occasion prompted A.P.H., who was adept in drawing up Bills for Parliament, real or imaginary, to draw up the following one:

INDUSTRIAL EFFICIENCY (TANGYE)

A
BILL

To secure and maintain the industrial efficiency and material prosperity of the realm, and for other purposes.

WHEREAS it is impossible, and indeed unworthy for any true Englishman to enjoy a sound, continuous and sufficient sleep under the same roof as JEAN EVERALD TANGYE, unless located in the same room, and accordingly, upon her visits to large centres of population, through the unrest and frustration of men of art, commerce and all lawful affairs much injury is done to the efficiency of the realm and the Queen's revenue.

And it is expedient that the presence of the said dangerous and disturbing influence should be kept secret.

Be it therefore enacted by the Queen's most Excellent Majesty by and with the advice of the Lords Temporal and Spiritual and Common, in this present Parliament assembled, and by the authority of the same as follows:—

1. (1) It shall be an offence to publish, reveal or disclose the presence of JEAN EVERALD TANGYE in any County Borough, Municipal Borough, or parish having a population exceeding ten persons.

(2) Not withstanding anything in the Hotels or Immigration Acts, no reference of the presence of JEAN EVERALD or DEREK ALAN TREVITHICK TANGYE shall be made in the books of any tavern, inn or hotel.

2. (1) This Act may be cited as the JEAN TANGYE ACT 1959.

(11) This Act shall come into operation forthwith.

(111) This Act shall apply to England, Wales, Scotland and Northern Ireland.

There were many letters from A.P.H. in Labour Warms. Scrawly writing, sometimes only decipherable with the aid of a magnifying glass. One summer Gwen his wife, and as good a friend to us as A.P.H., wrote asking whether we could have him to stay as he was badly needing a quiet holiday. Soon after his arrival, we were having breakfast one morning when he mentioned that he had no idea what to write next, a book or a play.

'Why not turn *The Water Gipsies* into a musical?' said Jeannie.

His novel, *The Water Gipsies*, a story about the canals, had been hugely successful many years before.

'Ah yes—' he began . . . and then, at that moment, there was a great squawking from the roof, and it was Hubert the gull of *A Gull on the Roof* crying out, beak to the heavens.

'There you are,' I said, 'Hubert approves!'

A month later A.P.H. completed the play and nervously set off from Minack to show it to Vivian Ellis, whose home

131

was at Minehead; and Vivian proceeded to compose a score which was as enchanting as the other scores he had written for *Big Ben, Tough at the Top* and *Bless the Bride*. A year later, we had this letter from A.P.H. at The County Hotel, Theatre Square, Nottingham:

August 4—1955

Jean, darling, and Derek,

Observe the date! It was August 4, 1954, that I wrote the first sketch of the scenes of W.G. and the fatal words 'Act One, Scene One.' And now, just a year later, I am writing to report that the little ship has been well and truly launched, thank God . . . and you! As you will see from the enclosed, it really did seem to please them on Tuesday, and I thought it was wonderful to get anyone there at all, as it is very hot and stuffy. Very many thanks for your letter and telegram. Gwen said: 'Who's Hubert?' I feel rather played out. After the first night Gwen gave a little party here but the blasted management insisted on having a 'conference' and broke it up. We argued about this and that till nearly 4 a.m. (whisky, etc. flowing pretty freely) but I get up feeling like H—— at 8 a.m. and at 9 was writing more verses! I may get home tomorrow, but I've got to come up to Manchester on Sunday.

The ghastly thing about this sort of tour is that it's a first night every Monday—culminating in that hideous business in London.

Well, bless you, and again 1001 thanks for your inspiration and support.

Much love from your exhausted Alan.

Jeannie and I were at the Winter Garden Theatre for the London first night and, when the curtain came down at the end of the performance, the audience rose applauding from their seats.

He continued periodically to stay with us and he was here when *A Gull on the Roof* was in manuscript, and he gave us much encouragement. He was here, too, when Charles Pick, the publisher, came to see me and, years later, it was Charles Pick who asked us to use our influence

with A.P.H. into persuading him to write his autobiography. He had written *Independent Member*, but that was
an account of his parliamentary days, and Charles Pick
wanted a book that would cover the whole expanse of his
life. It proved to be a mammoth book, requiring much
research and, every now and then, he would send us reports
on its progress. He became weary of it and yet his final
chapter *A Good Run* is one of the most evocative farewells
I have ever read. His remarks in the Preamble of the book
flattered Jeannie and me . . . though he mischievously
balanced them in the copy he gave us. In red ink he wrote:

> To Jean and Derek
> their 'bloody book'
> With love from Alan.

We were, it doesn't need me to say, greatly touched to
be asked to his eightieth birthday party at the Savoy. It
was a family affair and the invitation came from John, his
son, a director of Christie's, his daughters Crystal,
Lavender, and Jocelyn, who first won fame as a stage
designer at the Royal Court Theatre in London; and
Gwen. A half dozen guests, outside those of the family,
were present, and one of them of course was Vivian Ellis,
who came with Hermione his sister. After the dinner, after
the speeches, Vivian sat at the piano and played the songs
which A.P.H. loved. An elegant party and, when it was
over, A.P.H. took the red rose which he wore in his lapel
and gave it to Jeannie. She still has the petals. In a glass
jar with a silver top.

One never felt any age gap with him. He was always a
contemporary, and this was because he never talked
ponderously about age. At any age, he knew, one can be
foolish. At any age, too, one can be wise. No age has
an exclusive right to wisdom; and thus, possessing this
attitude that all ages are equal, he was as much in tune
with the young as with those of his own time.

Football pools were always a common ground with us

and he would conduct correspondence with Jeannie about his efforts to win the jackpot. He persevered in this attempt with dogged devotion, and went to the trouble of writing *Pools Pilot* which began with the introduction:

Some shallow thinkers may call this work dangerous; but that would be jumping to most unfair conclusions. True, we offer instructions to high and humble, peer and plumber, which may, or may not lead them to profits and gains, free of income tax. . . .

Despite, however, his perseverence, his research, his patience, he never did succeed in winning that hefty sum which, he said, would enable him to say as he was handed the £500,000 cheque: 'Me and my missus are going on just as before.'

Nor, of course, has Jeannie ever won it, although she has enjoyed one moment of triumph. It occurred when she checked her coupon on the Sunday before we travelled to London for A.P.H.'s Memorial Service at St Martin-in-the-Fields. On the previous Tuesday, when she was about to fill in the coupon, she looked up into the sky and said: 'Come on, Alan, help me with my coupon. Which teams shall I choose?'

Her entry scored 22 points; and she won £92.

The Memorial Service included a song, accompanied on the organ by Vivian Ellis, which came from *The Water Gipsies*. I remember A.P.H. writing the verses one sunny afternoon, sitting on the white seat beside the verbena bush opposite the barn; and I remember that the sound of the bells of Paul Church above Mousehole were being carried by the wind to Minack. This was the song:

> Peace and quiet, that's the thing.
> Here we hear the church bells ring.
> We can hear the lofty lark
> And the birds that love the dark.
> Water tumbling down the weir,
> Water whisp'ring 'sleep is here'—

Then the cock our waking clock
Softly calls across the lock.
Bells that ring, birds that sing,
Peace and quiet—that's the thing.

Ah little boat! One summer day
My love and I will sail away,
And hand in hand some better land discover.
Away, away, the seagulls cry,
The sail is set, the tide is high,
The winds blow free,
But where is he my lover.

The first verse is then repeated. It was a simple song
with a haunting melody; and those of us who were present
that morning at St Martin-in-the-Fields were deeply
moved. The *'Good Run'* had ended. Not that the ghost of
A.P.H. would have been sad himself. After the Service the
ghost would have suggested a visit to Joe Gilmore at the
Savoy Bar and then asked for a gin. A couple of gins later,
he might remark that he was beginning to feel unsea-
worthy and, if asked, he might quote a verse he spon-
taneously brought forth on his arrival one time at Hobart,
Tasmania. A reporter asked if he would write his own
epitaph. A.P.H. light-heartedly replied:

The demon gin what did me in
But bless the Lord who gave us gin.

Quite untrue, of course. He was naturally gregarious
and, because he 'gave', he was always fun to be with.

When my mother was ill I wrote a daily letter to her, not
out of duty, but out of a selfish wish to do so. My mother
was absorbed by the detail of our lives. Some of these
letters came back to me after she had died. Here are two
of them I found in Labour Warms. They concern the early
days at Minack:

February 5th

Darling, well here we are again and the snow is still on

the car and the lane impassable and the ground so hard that a pick-axe can't break it. A bitter North East near gale has been blowing and has been doing what the frost hasn't done already. The wallflowers have now gone beyond repair, the violets and the anemones are finished, and the marigolds, and I can scarcely believe that the forget-me-nots can recover.

One must look back eight months to last June to measure the tragedy. Then we were deciding where to put the anemones, the wallflowers, the violets and so on. In June we planted our first wallflower seed which within a month had disappeared as it had been eaten by flea beetle. So we toured the area trying to get plants, and calling on nursery-men at Camborne, Redruth, Helston, and we were very excited when we found them at a place at St Ives. We bought 2500 which we carefully planted, kept weeded, watching over them like growing children until last week they were beginning to flower. In June we had planted the 20,000 anemone corms. In June we had planted the violets . . . and ever since there has been weeding and weeding. Now they have all finished before their cropping time had hardly started.

Another letter dated August 21st, no year:

Darling, we are all set to go into town for the shopping and it is 8 a.m. We go early to escape the crowds and I am going in because we seem to have a holocaust of wire-worms and leather jackets on one part of the anemones. It really is a battle. The anemones in this part haven't been looking too good and yesterday we were weeding them and found these little bastards. So I am going into town to find something to deal with them.

Good heavens, my wife, my dear wife, has just come into the room in a new costume. A simple grey affair, with a white collar, and a woollen texture. So I have been able to say how lucky she is to have a husband who im-mediately notices such a purchase. She got it at Harrods: 'Just for a day like this . . .' which is cold and blustery like the beginning of November.

For myself I have on a pair of white linen trousers

which I got in Fiji. I have had no alteration to them and they fit perfectly. With jacket they cost thirty bob.

In the same corner of Labour Warms I found the file of correspondence my father kept during a tour of the world I made just before the 1939 war. He had kept all the letters I had written to my family and copies of the letters he wrote to me. I was close to my father although he was a man who found it difficult to communicate his true feelings to others. He and I used to go fly fishing for trout together along the winding Fowey river which runs below the railway line either side of Bodmin Road station; and though at the end of the day we would vividly discuss our fishing experiences, during the day while we were fishing we kept well apart. Each of us enjoyed the pleasure of being alone.

The letter I quote is one of those he wrote to me while I was staying in Tahiti and other islands of the South Seas; and as he himself had been to Samoa in his youth, he intuitively sensed my emotions. He always began his letters to me: 'My dear Cur'. A curious form of endearment. He was writing the letter from the family home Glendorgal, near Newquay:

My dear Cur, Your stay in Tahiti is fast nearing its close, and I have been thinking so much of you, for I can well understand your feelings, mingled with intense regret and yet the desire to get on. I am sure that you and I are kindred souls as regards our sentiments towards the South Seas, and your heartstrings will be torn just as much as mine, and those of the Bounty mutineers, and that of Rupert Brooke who heard 'the calling of the moon, and the whispering scents that stray, about the idle warm lagoon'. What a wonderful trip you are having. I never went to Tahiti to my lasting regret, but possibly you will be able to get a trader to Apia which I knew well. If you get there have a drink at the Tivoli Hotel on the beach, and look out for my ghost and any relatives. Possibly you may meet a man named Gurr there. He was R. L. Stevenson's solicitor. I bought some of Stevenson's books from him, and they are still in the library here.

I got the book by Robert Keable. Curiously enough I had never heard of it, ravenous though I am for any literature about the islands. What a strange career—parson, missionary, a Chaplain in France during the Great War, and ending his life with a native girl in far away Tahiti. I have found all the places both he and you mention on my German map, and so I can visualise all the spots alluded to. No wonder, on hearing the news from 'civilisation', you made up your mind to stay on in a carefree world; you were indeed wise to do so. But I fear that your return to 'civilisation' will be much in the nature of an anti-climax, for everything will seem so petty and sordid.

Aloha, farewell

I found in a corner of the cupboard a fan letter addressed to Jeannie about her book *Meet me at the Savoy*. A rather special fan letter for it came from Lady Juliet Duff, a legend of the Society world, a close friend of many of those distinguished men and women who belonged to the first part of the 20th century. Out of the blue came this letter:

Dear Mrs Tangye: I have only just read your book, and I want so much to write and tell you how enormously I enjoyed it. The Savoy has never lost its magic for me, since my childhood days in the nineties, when I used to hear of the De Reszkes, Melba, and Calvé staying there. (My mother and step father Lord and Lady De Grey were, with Harry Higgins, directors of the Covent Garden Opera.) I imagined it, I think, as a kind of fairy palace where only very special people stayed, and which if I were lucky I might someday see.

When, in later years, I first went there, it was to the Restaurant, *never* the Grill, for 'ladies' were not supposed to go to the Grill, and you will hardly believe it when I tell you, that in 1913, John Manners (killed alas very early in the War) was had up by his Colonel and sharply reproved for taking his twin sisters to supper there! Afterwards it was the place we loved best (in spite of the charm of Santarelli in the Restaurant), Manetta always made one feel as though one were a welcome guest at a private party, and I am sure that had one ever gone there to supper alone, he would have fixed one up, saying: 'Would you like to go to Lady Diana's table, or I'm sure Mr Kommer would like you to join his party.'

I *am* so glad you said what you did about the American correspondents and broadcasters—no one else that I can discover paid them the tribute which is their due. I've always felt that a monument as big as St Paul's ought to be put to them for what they did for us during those horrible days (as someone said, never were neutral correspondents less neutral). I didn't know them all, like you did, but I always think gratefully of Ed Murrow, Bill Stoneman, Helen Kirkpatrick, Walter Graebner, and of dear little Ben Robertson who was killed.

What fascinating years you had there, and I am sure you miss it in a way, though your present life does sound delightful, and I'm sure you wouldn't change it. Thank you again for a great treat, and if ever you are motoring to London, *do* look in on me here.

Juliet Duff.
Burbridge House,
Wilton, Salisbury.

We had several letters from her during the coming years, but we never met. It was a period when we never moved from Minack because we never had the funds to pay for a journey to London. After *A Cat in the Window* was published, she, a cat lover, wrote me a kind letter:

I hope you have another book in mind, for you must never stop writing. The other night at Noël's opening I found myself sitting next to A.P.H. and we talked a lot about you both.

A friend and I had already seen the play in Bristol on Whit Saturday, and brought Noël back here for the weekend, and he was as delightful as ever; and reminiscing, we realised it was just over forty years since we first met. The lady he wrote *The Vortex* about brought him over to see me in Kent, in a tiny house where I lived in those days, and we picked gooseberries, and he said 'you *do* think I'll be a success don't you?' He had already written *The Young Idea*, but of course *The Vortex* brought him right to the top; and the lady he'd written it about, a Mrs Foster, came to the opening, and was delighted with everything.

To return to *A Cat in the Window*—how I wish I had known him, and he must have been so much nicer than the Field Marshall. By the way, a few weeks ago he and I were both staying at Chartwell, and at dinner one night I asked him something, and called him Lord Montgomery. He said 'Oh don't call me Lord Montgomery, call me Field Marshall!'

Now can you help over this? In your first book you speak of the hotel your brother Nigel runs; would it do for Lady Churchill, or is it for the young and agile? Winston is going away, and she so terribly wants a rest, and she hates Brighton. She's coming here next week-end, then has to go back to Chartwell to deal with a large party of ladies from Winston's constituency, so it would be the following week. If you have a moment do write and tell me what you think, or if there is anywhere else that would do for her.

Juliet Duff.

Noël Coward usually sent telegrams to his friends, notes were comparatively rare. I was surprised to receive one after I had sent him a copy of *A Donkey in the Meadow*. There it was in Labour Warms, and I read it again:

My dear Derek,
I was entirely enchanted by *A Donkey in the Meadow*, and thank you so very much for sending it to me. Your writing is so lucid and gay, and I enjoyed every minute of it.
I love Fred and I love Lama, in fact I love the lot.
Thank you a million. . . . love Noël.

He had such gusto. In an area of the world which has much insincerity, he himself never failed to prove his integrity. Gertrude Lawrence said to me that she had never understood him, but she loved him for just being

Noël. I think she was a little scared of him, certainly she was anxious to have his approval of every part she played. But Gertie always needed boosting by someone. She was never secure.

A year before she died, she asked me to write her biography; and her letter was followed by one from her lawyer, Fanny Holtzmann, offering me trips to New York and Hollywood. Jeannie and I had just started our life at Minack and so I wrote back that we had made our decision to live here and we were not going to be deviated from it whatever the temptation to do so. 'Anyhow,' I added in my letter, 'you're too young for a biography.' A year later she died.

Now, having seen the movie *Star*, which had Julie Andrews playing Gertie, I wish I had written her biography; and perhaps my contract would have given me the chance to write the script of the movie. As it was, the movie seemed to me to be a disaster. There was no whisper of Gertie's devastating charm. No sign of her subtlety in singing a song. No hint of her wayward femininity. No evidence of the loyalty she gave to friends. No touch of the magic with which she entranced an audience. When watching the movie, I suddenly found myself thinking of Derby Day and, instead of the thoroughbreds racing into the straight from Tattenham Corner, I saw a trundling London bus.

I found several of her letters in Labour Warms, and here are extracts from two of them. The first is an example of a very insecure Gertie, full of wild hopes:

The Cape Playhouse,
Darlings,   Sept 17, 1949   Cape Cod
Please forgive me for not having written you before this, but things have certainly been on the jump since my return. What with rehearsals, problems, the heat, and suddenly finding myself extremely tired, I found there was no chance to write without falling asleep at the desk. Added to all this I was whisked off to New York after the

play at Dennis on the Saturday night to make a test for Warner Brothers. Jack Warner sent his own car and chauffeur and I went off all alone in the dark. We drove for seven hours through the night, arrived at 7 a.m. in New York where I was ushered (very secretly) into the most fabulous suite at Hampshire House, 3 bedrooms, 3 baths, kitchen and vast living room, overlooking Central Park. There I stayed for exactly one hour, and was then taken to the studios where I found Irving Rapper, the director and Carl Foynd the cameraman (both flown in specially from the Coast) plus 4 costumes, make-up men and wardrobe women. We worked without stopping to breathe until 7.15 p.m., by which time I felt as though I had been beaten up by bandits and left for dead. At the time I kept saying to myself 'Why am I doing all this?' and 'It's bound to be a flop anyhow, so why all the fuss?'. . . I flew back to the Cape at 8 a.m. on the Monday morning in time to rehearse again for the 2nd week of *September Tide* . . . well, days went by, the test had to be flown back to the Coast to be 'processed', and meanwhile I was certain it had all been a lot of time wasted. Then the avalanche began, and now deals have been made, contracts signed, and tonight in Hollywood Warner Brothers are throwing an enormous party for Tennessee Williams at which I am to be launched nation wide, like Vivien Leigh in *Gone With the Wind*.

So my dears, you have another film star on your hands for future accommodation—star of *Glass Menagerie*. Jane Wyman is playing the crippled girl, Kirk Douglas the son, and it is going to be Warner Brothers' prestige picture of the year, and they hope for the Academy Award, so maybe if I try very hard, which I shall, little 'Gee' may come home with an Oscar?

Devotedly,

Gee.

She didn't win an Oscar, though she won much praise for her performance of Amanda . . . though the Amanda of *The Glass Menagerie* was never as enchanting as the Amanda of *Private Lives*.

The second letter is the one she wrote after the opening in New York of *The King and I*. It was her great ambition to star at Drury Lane, but this was never to be. She died too soon.

April 1, 1951

Hello Darlings,

This is no April Fool's Day to me . . . we have got *the most terrific hit*.

Nothing has ever been produced on Broadway by anyone else that has in any way touched the public and the critics as has 'Anna'. I am sending you all the notices, and though we have only been open 3 days, I am *longing* to get the play to London . . . but we shall have to wait at least 3 years, as it looks now.

I think of you both even in my busiest and most nerve-racking days, and during the rehearsals and the road try-out, and I often envied your peaceful meadows. I shall be sending you some more packages of surprises now that all is calm again. . . .

You will go wild about the play. It is simply beautiful, touching, and most engaging and enchanting in every way, and I have had notices for my *singing*!! Have been studying for about 4 years since *Lady in the Dark*.

My love always,

Gee.

Gertie made a habit of these enthusiastic outbursts. Over-generous, over-extravagant, aiming to turn every occasion into one of drama and fun; she could, even in her personal relationships, imagine a goose to be a swan. When she died, the lights both of Broadway and Shaftesbury Avenue were dimmed . . . not even Gertie's enthusiasm could have expected such a tribute.

It proceeded to rain all day. A cup of coffee in the morning, sandwiches at lunch, a pot of tea in the afternoon, and I continued to delve into Labour Warms. Much of it was a waste of time, reading old newspapers, the reason for keeping which I couldn't remember, staring at photographs, tearing up long ago bills; and it was just when I was about to stop that I found a number of Jack Broadbent's letters.

He was an eccentric, a passionately loyal friend, and a newspaper correspondent who perceptively surveyed the world scene. Periodically he would suddenly appear at Minack after having flown from Washington, or Paris, or Rome; and I described in *Lama* the hilarious, though poignant as it turned out to be, time he came for Christmas. The last letter he wrote to me had vision, as well as humour. . . .

Want a bet? The Americans (as I told you years ago) will make a deal with the Russians before I lose the last of my hair, which won't be long. There is no such thing now as an Anglo-American alliance. They don't want to listen to us. Why should they? Our Empire has gone, and they have helped its destruction by their envy of it . . . but how mad I get about those who have been running the Empire. They have neglected that great prize year by year for a generation at least. The Tories are more to blame than anybody else though the real fault is fundamental. Whatever political party in power tried to rule the Empire on what were the domestic necessities of home politics.
Yet it will not be a bad thing for us, if we keep our heads. It can compel our people to face the facts. We have still a big part in the new world if we face facts and we have big enough men to act. If there is any imagination left in our would be leaders we are in for a good time. But if they are going to be the same bunch of stuffed shirts and other kinds of stupid people we shall sink lower and lower.
About you and Jeannie, however, I am certain as ever you are doing what you like best and enjoying it. The more I see of cities and capitals, aeroplanes and jets, ships and motor cars, restaurants and bars, idiots and cunning men, politicians and newspapermen, editors and newspaper pundits, columnists and criminals . . . you made the right decision at the right time. Timing, that's what's so important in life.

Three months after his Christmas stay with us, he was found dead in a Westminster flat he had temporarily rented. The two rooms were in disorder and a gilded mirror in the sitting-room was smashed. In January he had retired from the *Daily Mail* with a golden handshake and, in the company of an officer of a Guards regiment, haunted various fashionable gambling clubs. Towards the end of March he told a friend that the Guards officer owed him a great deal of money. Whether this was an excuse to cover up his own losses, I do not know. All I can say is that the barman at the block of flats wrote to me (I had never met him) saying that he had something important to tell me; and he wished to tell me personally.

The next time I went to London, I set off one lunchtime to see the barman. I never saw him. He had died the week before.

So I will never know what happened to Jack Broadbent . . . though he was up there on the roof when I finished my session with Labour Warms.

TEN

My resolution to withstand domination by the donkeys was a fiasco, I am afraid, from the beginning.

I would slip out of the back door if they were in a position to see me coming out of the front, and slip out of the front door if they could see me coming out of the back . . . and then set off on a walk of my own. Or, if they were in the stable field in front of the barn, thus barring my normal route to the cliff, I would go up the three steps to Lama's field, turn left past the corner where we have built a stone hedge topped with earth and full of flowers, and down another few steps into the $QE2$ field. Then I would scurry or, more likely, Jeannie and I both would be scurrying along the top-side of the field until we reached the far end where we would slide down a steep bank into one of our top cliff meadows. We would then believe we were free.

Freedom would be brief. The donkeys' acute hearing would catch the sound of our hasty footsteps or, if they were placed in the right situation, they would catch a glimpse of us as we sneaked away; and thereupon they would set up a heartrending hullabaloo and the sound of it would make us feel sorry for them. After hesitation, and an urgent talk, we would retrace our steps, unlatch the gate, fasten on the halters, and start on our walk again . . . except now there were four of us.

I had also, on that New Year's Day, been determined to withstand another form of pressure which they regularly put on us. They had two main grazing grounds, the stable field in front of the barn and the donkey field above the cottage; and if they had become bored in one, they would make it plain that they wanted to move to the other. They would stand, heads side by side, looking over one or other of the gates, pawing occasionally at the ground and displaying their impatience, sometimes whinnying, sometimes hee-hawing, until at last I would say to Jeannie: 'We had better move them.'

Such a decision would seem to imply that there was now only the simple procedure of putting on their halters and leading them up the path from the stable field or down the path from the donkey field. This was not so. As soon as they realised they had successfully imposed their wishes upon us, as soon as we had reached the gate, halters in hand, one or other of them, or both, would play a maddening trick upon us. Instead of meekly standing, waiting for the halters to be fastened, they would turn their bottoms to us and walk away. Or, if Penny were compliant, pushing her head forward so that there was no problem in fixing the halter, Fred, perversely, would scamper away as I approached him.

'Fred!' I would shout. 'Fred! Come here!'

This, he thought, was hilariously funny; a quirky humour which I did not find funny at all. In disgust I would take Penny by the lead, walk out through the gate and shut it; and thereupon Fred would race across the field and slide to a stop at the gate, as if he were daring to say: 'Hey, you're leaving me behind!' This impression, however, was just a trick, a device to annoy me again . . . for when I had pulled back Penny to the gate and opened it, halter in my hand, Fred would dash away again, leaving me to fume. Penny also, from time to time, would make me fume. Penny would behave in the same fashion. She would dance away when I approached her, kicking her heels,

148

putting her head down as if she were laughing, while Fred with halter in place, lead in my hand, would tolerantly watch her antics. For both, such behaviour was a means of bringing spice to the day.

One might suppose that, once they had their halters in place, the act of leading them from field to field would also be a simple affair. Once again, one would be wrong. When, for instance, we led them from the stable field up past the cottage to the donkey field, there was always one particular point near a rock and few yards from our bedroom window where each would anchor their four feet. It was a ritual. Without fail, every time they reached this point, they would come to a full stop.

'Come on! Come on!'

And they would refuse to move.

Perhaps they acted in this way as a joke, although their faces did not suggest this. When they were joking it was easy to see they were doing so by their manner, but when they came to a full stop on the path, they seemed to be adopting a bolshy attitude. As if they were saying: 'We're as good as them. They may feed us and look after us, and without them we don't know where we would be . . . but we are going to prove that we have the power. If we don't want to move, they can't make us.'

If these were their thoughts, they fortunately did not persist with them. We would tug, cajole, shout a few epithets, and they would proceed; but there was now another hazard. We had to steer them between the flower beds which bordered the path, steer them from taking a mouthful of nicotiana, or of antirrhinums, or of marigolds, or alyssum, or pansies, or rudbeckia, or any other of the flowers I had grown so hopefully in the spring. Then, when they had reached the corner of the cottage which leads to the porch there was the huge escallonia on the one side and, on the other, the fragrant tree-like bush with feathery green leaves and tiny white flowers, the name of which I do not know. These flowers and bushes were nectar to the

149

donkeys. They lunged at them as we passed. We pulled them away. They lunged again. The short walk from stable field to donkey field and back was always an adventure.

The flowers they lunged at, however, had not bloomed as successfully as I had hoped. It was easy to find excuses . . . there had been a persistent cold wind soon after I had planted them out from the seedboxes, and then came a hot spell that dried our shallow soil into the texture of sand. We watered and watered, pumping from the small reservoir whose main purpose was to supply the greenhouses, but as I stood, hose in hand, splashing the small plants, I knew there was no body in the soil to hold it. Hence I realised that the trouble was largely of my own making. Back in the winter, long before I became excited about my seedlings, I should have first prepared the soil and put heart in it. They were all small beds around the cottage of the rockery type, and so I should have treated each one as a flower pot.

Many of the plants, therefore, disappeared without any aid from Penny and Fred; and all the cosseting I provided did not save the Sunshine Calceolaria Rugosa. Splendid, firm little plants in the box, they began to wilt as soon as I put them out. I fussed over them like a nanny. I watered them, fed them with liquid manure and, when they continued to show no signs of recovering, I regretfully found myself becoming angry. Only too late did I realise what was the real trouble. Leather jackets, those squishy inch-long grubs which turn into daddy-long-legs, were eating the roots.

I am not, therefore, a good gardener. I should have foreseen all these problems; though there were successes to report. The cosmea, the balsam and the salvia were failures because the slugs ate them, but the Crystal Palace lobelia were a glorious dark blue; and the Suttons Triumph antirrhinums gave a wonderful first display and, when this was finished, I gave the dead blooms a haircut, and so prepared the way for a second, even better, display. Little sign of the Cambridge Blue lobelia, however, and no sign at all of Rosie O'Day, the deep rose pink alyssum. The Snowdrift alyssum became brown patches during the hot spell but, when the rains came, it soon burst into white and this was a lesson. Alyssum needs continuous drenching if it is to flower.

The nicotiana were a success so long as one looked at them in the evening, in the early morning, or on a very dull day. Their scent then was gorgeous, and so were the pink and white flowers, but when the sun shone the petals withered and the plants became bedraggled, looking as if they should have been thrown on the compost heap; and I would apologise for them: 'You should see them at night!' I would say brightly to anyone who seemed to be gazing at them in disapproval.

The sunflowers, too, were a success and so were the Blue Blazer ageratum. The sunflowers were such a success that they grew tall enough for a child to be hoisted on to my shoulders in order to look at the great dinner plates of the flowers; and they were much admired until a September gale blew them down. I salvaged the dinner plates and brought them into the greenhouse because, from the beginning, I had hoped they would provide seeds for the wild birds. Not a hope. It was to be a wet autumn and there was no sun to ripen them.

The Blue Blazer ageratum was a modest little flower, and it edged the border of a new bed we had made, siding the lane close to Monty's Leap; and there were clusters of it elsewhere, and it gave pleasure all through the summer. But the seed of my New Year resolution which proved to be my triumph was rudbeckia. Wherever I had put out the plants they blossomed into great daisy-type flowers of orange with mahogany centres and they brought colour to the garden when, I have to confess, my own contribution had, for the most part, failed.

As for Jeannie, my efforts helped to confirm her distrust of annuals. She is a perennial believer. She accepts that certain annuals are well worth growing, but believes that anyone with a small garden who relies on them is asking for trouble. Hence, although she showed sympathy, she also felt self-justified; and the blank corners of the garden supported her. Perennials, she argued, dig their roots deep into the ground and are immune to droughts and strong enough to withstand early spring cold winds.

My complaint about perennials is that they spread, smothering everything around them. Hence a Michaelmas daisy, for instance, will envelop a corner of our garden, produce its flowers at the appropriate time, but be a great chunk of non-flowering plant for the rest of the year. A tidy gardener would, no doubt, keep it under control, but Jeannie has such a love for all plants, suitable or unsuitable, that she can never bring herself to be ruthless enough to deal with them. Jeannie can never throw anything away. Our strawberry plants had a virus, but she wanted to keep the remnants of them. I once had a ton of bulbs which the Ministry of Agriculture Advisory Officer advised me, because of their condition, to throw into the sea. Not a chance. Jeannie was determined to keep them. She was convinced that, in some miraculous way, they would recover. They didn't.

Her particular success this summer lay in her nurturing of the geranium cuttings which she had planted out in the greenhouse the previous autumn. Along one side of the Orlyt in front of the cottage was a splendid bed of geraniums, deep red ones and pink ones. They had all so enjoyed their winter quarters that they had grown long stalks, thus becoming elongated geraniums. Nonetheless, they had already earned their occupation of the greenhouse by providing cut blooms for the cottage and now, suddenly, they were available for another role; and this was to fill the vacant places caused by the failure of my cosseted annuals.

Giraffe-like geraniums, therefore, were now dug up from the Orlyt by Jeannie and transported to various barren spots in the garden, and carefully planted and watered in. A splash of red, or pink, now lit up the barren spots and so it remained until the geranium realised what had happened . . . that it was no longer leading a sheltered life in the greenhouse and that, in middle age, it had been suddenly thrust into reality. The leaves would then yellow, the blooms droop, and I would say to Jeannie that it would have been much better if she had left the geraniums where they were happy. In time, though, I was to be proved wrong. The giraffe-like geraniums acclimatised themselves to their new, tough situation; and colourfully filled the gaps my annuals had created.

We have, of course, always to be on guard against plants, bushes or trees which are poisonous for donkeys. Yew is a killer, and rhubarb, and Russell lupins. We once had a kind person give us two small eucalyptus trees and we planted them in the wood close to the hut where Boris, our Muscovy drake, had lived. Penny and Fred were once allowed to wander in this small wood, but were stopped when we realised that they were treating the bark of the trees as a delicacy and that, therefore, the trees were in danger.

The 'Verboten' sign, however, which we put up, our refusal to let them go anywhere near the small wood, both annoyed and intrigued them. Fred, in particular, was fascinated as to why the one-time access was now denied him. Whenever we went with him on an aimless stroll, halter around his head, the lead in my hand, and we neared the gap which led to the wood, he would strain to go there. One day he *did* go there, and it was my fault that he did so.

I had been giving rides on Fred and Penny to two children and, after these were over, the two children asked if they could see Oliver and Ambrose. I said of course if we could find them, and I immediately began to wonder where they might be and, thereupon, I forgot the donkeys. When I ushered the children out of the gate in the donkey field above the cottage, I foolishly left it ajar behind me. The donkeys did not notice my mistake for an hour or more. The children had gone and I was weeding the roses, when Jeannie called out the news that the donkeys were in the wood. The wood where the donkeys were banned; where there was my mythical 'Verboten' sign; where the two eucalyptus trees were, unfortunately, planted. Fred, in his excitement to be where he shouldn't be, proceeded to gulp them.

We have all been in such a situation at some time in our lives when we have been tempted to indulge in some pleasure which should either have been totally ignored or treated with moderation. We have learnt from such experiences out of the misery of the after-effects. Fred learnt the same way.

The two eucalyptus trees gave him a hangover that he will remember for ever.

Donkeys, of course, are always pitting their wits against their owners; always, like long-term prisoners, plotting to escape. The donkeys mean no harm, nor are they wishing to prove they are hard done by. It is a kind of chess game they want to win. Penny and Fred, therefore, would contemplate as they stood motionless in a corner of a field as to how they could defeat our methods of incarcerating them.

Fred, for instance, would heave his bottom against the gate which led down towards the cliff in an attempt to open it; and so I countered by stringing barbed wire across it so that the next time he heaved, it hurt. Then there was the small white-painted gate close to the barn. The gate was made of stakes from a wreck, as was the fence either side of it, and the gate was fastened by a conventional bolt with a knob which was dropped into a slot when we closed the gate.

Fred must have watched us drop the knob on many occasions . . . until at last the idea dawned on him that if he were able to lift the knob upwards with his teeth and then shift the bolt until it was free of the catch on the fence, the gate would open for him. This trick, in due course, he perfected; and the day he achieved it, there was very nearly a disaster.

One morning I looked out of the bedroom window and saw the gate was open.

'We shut the gate last night, didn't we?'

'I saw you fasten it.'

'Well, it's open now!'

'Oh heavens, that means they're out!'

'Come on, hurry, we have to find them!'

This is never easy. I have seen them careering along the Coastal Path towards Carn Barges and, though thankful to have seen them, have wondered how to catch them. I have known them join the cows of Jack Cockram, my neighbour, and then find them heading the parade of cows as they were called in for milking. I have found them hiding in one of our small cliff meadows, or I have discovered them in the moorland on the other side of the shallow valley. There are any number of places they can escape to, where they can munch strange grass, where they can relish the devilment of their escape, where, in their opinion, they can enjoy freedom, be amused by our shouts as we look for them, knowing all the time that, in due course, we would find them and take them back to the comfort of their normal surroundings.

We have, however, one dominating fear when they escape. It may be irritating to find them on Carn Barges or, after a period of searching, in a cliff meadow, or somewhere on the moorland, but it also produces a sense of great relief. Our dominating fear is that they might, once they have made their escape, gallop down our mile-long lane to the main road. The thought of this horrifies us; and thus we have a plan that, whenever the alarm is raised of their escape, one of us always hastens to search up the lane, while the other sets off around the moorland.

On this occasion, it was I who went up the lane and,

from past experience, I expected that if they had gone this way I would find them mooching around the farm buildings at the top of the hill; or, if Jack Cockram, or Walter Grose, or Bill Trevorrow had seen them, I would expect to find them corralled in a field. These three were always ready to break off from their farm work to stop the donkeys from going any further, but when I reached the farm buildings I saw neither donkeys nor human beings. All was quiet. Everyone was out, and so there had been no one to see the donkeys pass by; and that is what had happened. I walked on a few yards until I was at the spot where I could look down the farm-to-main-road part of the lane and saw, in the far distance, Penny and Fred.

I had no time to go back and fetch Jennie and clearly there was no one around to help me cut them off; and cut them off I had to do, or else within a few minutes they would be on the road. 'Dear Derek,' I said to myself, 'keep calm, work out a plan, control your panic . . .'—and I was in a panic, because I knew that if I ran down the lane after them they would only rush onwards. In fact, I would only be a means of hurrying them into danger.

I had, therefore, to be stealthy. I observed from a distance that they had paused by some tasty hedge greenery at a point where the lane zig-zagged out of view. It was late May time, pleasant juices were in leaves and stalks, and this, I realised, was in my favour. It they did not see me, if I were so inconspicuous that they continued to nibble and chew the hedge delights, I could cut them off from the main road; and so it seemed that the best thing I could do was to run through the fields parallel to the lane, my head low, silent, a guerrilla in action, though on a peaceful mission instead of one bred on hate.

I let myself into the first field, knowing that I had six hundred yards and two further fields before I would be able to be between the donkeys and the main road; and I immediately ran into trouble when I reached the second field. It was waist-high in fine grass, all ready to be cut for hay. I dared not run along the narrow gap between the grass and the hedge for fear that the donkeys might hear me, and set off again; and so I had to risk being seen, being shouted at by the irate owner of the field, as I floundered through the grass, leaving a flattened trail behind me.

I reached the far hedge, climbed over it, and now found myself in a field of growing corn; and as I knew that I had reached a position which was nearly parallel to where the donkeys had paused, I stopped running and began to creep. I aimed to climb over the hedge siding the lane about twenty yards below the donkeys, but when I arrived at my chosen spot I found the hedge was topped by a mass of blackthorn. Any moment, I realised, the donkeys would be moving on. Penny would lead, I guessed. She was always the bold one on these safaris. Fred organised the break-out, Penny took over thereafter, and I had to get through the blackthorn before she set off again at the gallop.

A minute later I was on top of the hedge with black-thorn scratching my legs, scratching my face, scratching my hands and arms . . . and down below me, a few yards to my left, was an artful Penny and behind her an astonished Fred. What was *he* doing there? Ears pricked, a hee-haw at the ready, but Fred was not prepared for the reaction of Penny. His attitude seemed to be one of 'all is discovered', and he appeared willing to accept an unconditional surrender. Not so Penny.

Penny, sensing my entangled predicament amongst the blackthorn, was watching me carefully, wondering whether to make a dash. At that instant, if she had so acted, she would have won. She would have had a free run to her destiny on the main road . . . but, for a second, she hesitated and that was enough time for me. I made one last bleeding scramble through the blackthorn, took a flying leap to the lane, and held up my arms wide like a policeman on traffic duty. The wild adventure was over. Two donkeys who had chased danger were meekly on their way home . . . and to a new latch on the gate which, I hope, will for ever defeat the intelligence of Fred.

I was unable to keep my resolution to be free of donkey domination for the same reason that I was unable to keep my resolution to be free of cat domination. Every day I was involved in them. Every day, despite their often independent moods, I was made aware that they were a part of our lives. They were not pets. They did not belong to that category of unfortunate animal or bird or exotic snake which are bought by people as if they were manufactured toys and then discarded. We were all at one. It is not a kind of attitude that some people can appreciate. Magic does not exist for them; and it is magic which brings an animal and a human being together in mutual understanding. The animal trusts; and the human being sees in the animal the qualities he would like to see in his fellow human beings.

A consequence of such a relationship can be over-imaginative concern about the welfare of the animal, a form of hypochondria; and if I am in a certain mood, if I am tired or something has distressed me, I can suffer from over-imaginative concern. On the other hand, I am glad I feel as I do because I am constantly amazed by the casualness of others. I do not understand, for instance, those who allow a dog to wander the streets on its own, or a man I often see taking his dog for a walk along a busy country road where there is no pavement, without the dog being on a lead. Nor do I understand those who are so insensitive as to allow a dog to bark incessantly, thus ruining the peace of others. I am not blaming the dog for these things. I am blaming the owners.

Then there are the strange breed of people who indulge in dogs and cats as presents at Christmas-time. We all know examples of what happens. A puppy or a kitten is given as a present, producing ecstatic cries around the Christmas tree, games are played all through the holiday and into the New Year, and the puppy believes he has found his heaven. By the end of the month, however, the novelty has worn off, the puppy or kitten becomes more and more inconvenient, its owners have no space in their lives to love it, and so they begin to plan how to be rid of it . . . dump it at a stranger's door? Take it a car ride and drop it in some faraway countryside? Drown it perhaps, or leave it at night outside an Animal Home without leaving any money for its upkeep? Is such callousness the result of a society so obsessed by materialistic doctrines that it is blind and deaf to the magical pleasures? It seems so.

Penny causes me over-imaginative concern from time to time. She once nearly died from an attack of laminitis, a severe inflammation of the feet, and as this affliction can always recur, I am constantly on the watch for it. She has, however, a habit of giving me false alarms. She will stand still for an hour or more in the middle of the donkey field above the cottage, shifting her feet as if in discomfort, head down, looking lugubrious, until at last I am compelled, because of my anxiety, to walk over to her and murmur sweet nothings to her. She enjoys this attention and when, in order to test her true condition, I give her a gentle slap on the bottom to make her walk and so see whether she has difficulty in doing so, she replies to my solicitude by setting off at a gallop: 'I've fooled you again!' she seems to be inferring. Of course I am delighted . . . except on one occasion, of which I will soon tell.

Fred, however, startled me one day when I saw him standing in a corner of the field holding the right front leg off the ground; and it dangled as if a fetlock had been broken. It was lunch time. After breakfast, we had led him and Penny up from the stable field, where they had spent the night, and I had noticed nothing wrong. I had, therefore, no reason to guess why he was behaving so oddly, and when I crossed the field to him I gained no clue. He was looking sorrowful enough, let me rub his ears, his head down so that his white nose was touching the grass, allowed me to feel his dangling foot without objection, giving me the impression all the time that he wanted me to realise that he was a brave but very sick donkey. The impression, however, could also have been a ploy. In the past it was Penny who had always received the vet's attention; and I had often observed that Fred, while the attention was in progress, would shuffle round a few yards away making token bites at the grass, eyeing Penny and the vet a little jealously. He would like the vet's attention too. He was to receive it.

An hour after lunch I was saying to Jeannie that I was really worried. Fred had not moved a pace since I had been with him. He just stood close to the wood with his bottom to the trees, head lowered, right foot dangling.

'I'm going to 'phone the vet,' I said.

This is not a simple task. I have to drive the car, because we have no wish to be on the telephone, three miles to the nearest telephone box; and the vet has to drive six miles from his headquarters in Penzance. Thus one does not want to telephone unless the matter is truly serious, for vets, like doctors, are busy enough without being called out for trivial reasons.

'I'm sure you're right *this* time,' said Jeannie.

She was referring to the occasion, a few weeks before, when I was *not* delighted that Penny had fooled me.

She had been for a day or so in what we call her Connemara mood, as if she were spending the day dreaming of her younger days in the Connemara hills amid bogs and tinkers, and a colleen or two who had put their arms around her neck before she set off in a cattle truck for her travels across the Irish Sea to Exeter where she was auctioned, and to Wadebridge, and to the Plume of Feathers at Scorrier, and to Minack. In such a mood, she was desultory. In such a mood, she would stand at the far end of the field ignoring us while we stood at the gate calling her, offering her chocolate biscuits, or carrots, or potato crisps. Fred did not mind this mood. He ate the chocolate biscuits, the carrots, the potato crisps all by himself.

160

This particular morning, Jeannie had driven into Penzance early. We had already, of course, been to see Penny and she seemed to be in a deeper Connemara mood than ever, standing at the far end of the field and not bothering to move as we came towards her. This worried us. Fred was capering around, but Penny was still.

An hour after Jeannie had left, I had a look at her again, and there she was lying down on the ground, head on the grass, and the sight gave me a twinge of anxiety. When I reached her, however, she began to move, began to struggle to get up . . . front legs straightened, a heave of the body propelled by the back legs, and then a slow unwieldy effort to be upright. I put my arm round her neck and talked to her. Then I said: 'Come on, Penny, let's go a walk across the field.' She did not move. I gave her a gentle slap, and she still did not move. I gave her another one, and another one, and at last she hobbled a few feet. It was agony to watch. She could not put her back foot to the ground, it was as if she were half-paralysed; and she proceeded to make my distress even worse by turning her head, black ears lowered, and looking at me with such mournful eyes that it seemed she was saying goodbye to me. It was pitiful.

Clearly I had to get the vet to see her as soon as possible but, since Jeannie had the car, I had to borrow the telephone of one of the farms at the top of the hill. I never liked doing so, but it was an emergency, and I knew they would not mind; and so I left Penny to be miserable on her own, and hastened up the lane.

I met Bill Trevorrow coming down, his old Flossie at his heels.

'Something seriously wrong with Penny,' I said. 'Can I use your 'phone to ring the vet?'

'Go ahead. The missus is in . . . what's happened?'

'She can't walk.'

A few minutes later I passed Walter Grose. Walter, whose family of cats of all shapes and sizes, of all mixtures of colours gather around his van while he has his sand-wiches. Walter has worked one of the farms most of his life though he lives in St Buryan.

'Penny poorly? I'm sorry about that.'

'I thought it best to get the vet as soon as possible.'

I was sorry in a way that I had seen either Bill or Walter. I prefer secrecy in illness, animal or human . . . but now I was broadcasting Penny's distress.

'It could be thrush,' said Walter. 'That's rot in her foot. It's a difficult job to cure.'

Soon I was at Mrs Trevorrow's and I rang the vet, and the girl said someone would come as soon as possible. I returned down the lane, passing no one this time, until I reached Minack and the field where I had left Penny.

She was grazing beside Fred; and I was surprised by her apparent normality.

An hour later, Jeannie returned, and I told her what had happened. I described the pain that Penny so clearly demonstrated she was suffering from. Then I added, puzzled: 'She seems to be better. She seems to be able to walk.'

Occasions sometimes occur when a sector of oneself would like a bad thing to happen. You have, for instance, rung the police to report you have seen a suspicious character around, and when the police arrive you hope that your suspicions are confirmed; or you ring the fire brigade because of a frying pan blaze in the kitchen, then find yourself, against your will, hoping that it won't go out before the fire brigade arrives; or you see a holiday-maker in difficulties in the sea, race to give a 999 call, then reluctantly hope that the helicopter which is soon on the scene has not wasted its time.

Thus with the vet and Penny.

As hour by hour went by and the vet did not come, I watched Penny apprehensively as she became more and more normal.

Then at last a small white car came hurrying down the

lane, stuttered to a pause at Monty's Leap, then revved up again to rush to a full stop by the barn.

Out jumped not one vet, but three.

'Sorry I'm late,' said the vet I knew. 'We've been operating on a cow.'

He was fair-haired and eager, and he had a natural kindness which gave confidence. He was also making me feel how grateful I would be if there were a hole in the ground I could hide in. I had seen Penny. My apprehension had been confirmed. She was in the stable field looking alert; looking as if she were the healthiest donkey in the district.

She had fooled me again. A major fooling; and I was not amused.

The visit of the vet to Fred, however, was a different story.

ELEVEN

Fred had an abscess in his hoof, the hoof of his right foreleg; and it was so painful that he could not even take pleasure in the fuss that was made of him.

'What's up with him?'

Bill Trevorrow had come down the lane and was standing by the wall adjoining the barn.

'A flint from the chippings got wedged in his foot,' I said, 'and the vet says it's like having an abscess under the nail of your finger.'

'He looks bad.'

'Sometimes when I'm moving the two of them from the top field down here I don't put a halter on Fred. I put one on Penny, lead her down here, and then a minute or so later Fred follows at speed, travelling so fast that he slides to a stop. That's how he collected the flint.'

Fred was standing dejected a few yards away.

'Saw him when I was with the steers,' said Bill, 'and I could see something was wrong. That's why I came down.'

The steers were in the fields on the other side of the shallow valley. We kept an eye on them, just as Bill kept an eye on the donkeys; and when, on one occasion, we noticed a steer had lain still in the middle of a field for an hour or more while his companions had roamed off elsewhere, Jeannie hastened up to the farm to tell Bill. A false alarm, as it turned out, but Bill was grateful that we had troubled. And now I was grateful that he had troubled about Fred.

'The abscess will have to burst,' I said, 'before he gets better.'

'It'll have to do that all right.'

'Meanwhile, the vet's told us to bathe it twice a day in warm water and Dettol.'

'How does Fred take to that?'

'He doesn't.'

The vet had said that we should fill a bucket with the Dettol and warm water, then persuade Fred to stand his leg in it. The vet had spoken as if the deed were as easy as giving Fred a carrot. Fred, however, when he saw the bucket, reared like a bronco.

'Tell you what,' said Bill. 'Get Geoffrey to catch hold of his foot and then pour the Dettol into the hoof . . . and if you want any help, let me know.'

There were other offers of help. A small girl on holiday from Birmingham said she would come every day and stroke him, saying the stroking might take his mind off the pain. Leslie, who keeps the post office at St Buryan and who, when Fred had birthday parties, provided the ice-cream, sent him a carton of vanilla ice-cream. Our friend the Vicar of Marazion called and commiserated and, no doubt, offered a prayer. And all the while Fred remained miserable.

Penny, too, fussed over him, keeping him company, never straying far away from his lugubrious figure; and Oliver and Ambrose showed their interest, if not concern, by regularly sitting on the wall watching the treatment of Dettol and warm water.

After a week, and two further visits from the vet, there were signs of improvement. A wellwisher brought him a bunch of carrots, and after a first doubtful nibble he ate the lot. Chocolate biscuits were next day on the menu, then a packet of potato crisps and, finally, as a signal that his suffering was over, came the sudden colossal hee-haw from the centre of the field.

A sock, however, played an important part in his recovery. After the first treatment of Dettol and warm water, it became obvious that his foot had to be protected or else it would be sure to collect dirt. A bandage was out of the question, and I didn't care for another suggestion of wrapping polythene around it, for fear that Fred might bite it and swallow the pieces. It was then I had my idea about the sock. I was wearing a garish yellow pair which I had been given, and the thought suddenly occurred to me that here was the answer.

'Fred!' I said, though at that time he was too sick to respond. 'I'm going to give you a sock.' And I promptly took one off and a few minutes later it was on his foot.

It was at first just a useful covering but later, as he improved, he began to take a fancy to it. A garish yellow sock gave him a distinction. It was as if he knew that such a sight on a donkey was unusual and was certain to cause comment; and it *did* cause comment. Mirth too. A donkey wearing a yellow sock was a reason for laughter.

Meanwhile, Oliver and Ambrose had been consolidating their places on the bed and, since my resolution banning them from such comfort was now in tatters, I was wise enough to accept my defeat with grace. I was also influenced by the fact that Ambrose was prepared to offer such a sign of affection, because in daytime he continued to be often on edge and elusive. If I saw him outside and went to pick him up, he would still, more often than not, dart away from me; and when sometimes he copied Oliver, turning on his back, displaying his tummy to the skies and apparently inviting me to touch him, he would jump to his feet and run as soon as I was close to him. It was maddening . . . and yet the moments were increasing when he tantalisingly gave me hope that he was changing into a normal loving cat like Monty or Lama or Oliver. One morning after breakfast, for instance, he jumped on to my lap uninvited for the very first time in his life. I was astonished. I sat there immobile, Ambrose overflowing across my lap from cushion to cushion, and called for Jeannie to come and witness such a unique occasion.

Nevertheless, although there were such signs that he was improving his daylight manners, it was at night on the bed that he relaxed in our company. I would be awakened by Oliver purring on my chest, a whisker length away from my face, while Ambrose, also purring loudly, was spreadeagled across my feet pinioning them to the mattress; and, because I was accepting my defeat with good grace,I did nothing to disturb either of them.

I recognised the fact that I was their prisoner; and I refrained from shifting my leg just a little bit in order to give it relief because I feared that in retaliation they might both jump off the bed and I did not want that. I preferred the purring chains. I preferred to accept the compliment that they had chosen me as the site for sleep rather than the hay in the barn, the sofa in the sitting-room, or the expanse of the spare bed. Thus I would lie there in the dark, yearning to bend my knees, stretch, turn to one side or the other, kick my legs in freedom; and foolishly choosing not to do so for fear of interrupting the purring pleasures of two cats who had broken my New Year resolution.

The purrs of Ambrose were more prolonged than those of Oliver. Oliver was inclined to purr in short bursts, sudden moments of love of great intensity; while Ambrose was a long distance purrer; and indeed his purrs were of such duration that I would go to sleep listening to them, wake up perhaps a couple of hours later, and still be listening to them. Purring on the bed at night was for him as natural as breathing.

This persistence, however, sometimes irritated Oliver. It kept him awake, as a distant barking dog might keep me awake. Thus, at some stage, he would lose patience and I would be startled from my slumber by an explosion of cat temper. Oliver had hit Ambrose with a paw; and I would then hear a sleepy voice beside me: 'Stop it, you two. Stop those fisticuffs!' There would then be silence for a while as they settled down again . . . only for Ambrose in due course to start purring again.

Occasionally they would both act as if they were the guardians of our bedroom. The window which served as their entrance faced the lane running down to Monty's Leap; and in Monty's and Lama's time we used to fix a wire contraption in the open window to prevent them from going out at night . . . because Monty was a Londoner without experience of foxes and badgers, while Lama was small and vulnerable and we were happier knowing she was safe indoors.

Oliver and Ambrose, on the other hand, could look after themselves and, in any case, on the two occasions we did put up the contraption, Oliver knocked it down from the outside when wanting to come in, and made such a noise in doing so that we decided to give up the idea, and the contraption now lies on the floor under the bed.

One night I was lying awake while Ambrose was purring away at the the bottom of the bed and Oliver lying close enough for me to put my hand on him, and I was wondering about certain *oughts* with which we were faced. *Ought* is the word we use for those things we have an irking sense we ought to do, but don't want to do. They cover a wide area of activities.

'I *ought* to write to so-and-so.'

'We *ought* to accept the invitation.'

'As I'm going nearby, I *ought* to go and see them.'

'This a function we really *ought* to go to.'

'We haven't seen them for so long, we *ought* to ask them.'

The maddening thing about *oughts* is that they often operate both ways without those concerned being aware of it. Thus the person you felt you *ought* to invite only accepts, did you but know it, because he feels he *ought* to accept. Or, if you go to a party, are tired and want to go home, but do not do so because you feel you *ought* to stay longer, this is equalled by the behaviour of your host and hostess, who are only remaining with you because they feel they *ought* to.

I was thinking about certain of my current *oughts* when suddenly there was a commotion on the bed and the two cats, deep in slumber at one moment, had catapulted themselves on to the window-sill at the next. There was a full moon and it was very still; no noise except the perpetual murmur of the sea.

'I bet it's a fox,' I whispered to Jeannie, who was also awake.

Periodically a fox will investigate our dustbins, pushing off the lids so that they clatter noisily when they hit the ground. I lay waiting for the clatter. Not a sound.

But at the window Oliver and Ambrose were frozen, like two sentries, guns at the ready. This was a crisis. Clearly there was danger outside, or a threatening mystery, otherwise they would not have stayed so still. They would have jumped out of the window.

'Do you hear that strange noise?' I said softly.

Silence. Then there it was again. A crackly crunching.

'I'm going to have a look,' I whispered to Jeannie, and stealthily got out of bed and went to the window. I knelt there, Oliver on one side of me, Ambrose on the other, all three of us staring out of the window into the moonlight.

A crackly crunch.

The grey rocks and the old stones of the barn are ethereal in moonlight. It is a fairyland where pixies might suddenly appear; and the lane leading to Monty's Leap is touched with silver and, if you are in the mood to do so, you see the ghosts of past inhabitants of Minack, of old horses and cattle, of carts and haywains, and you regain in your imagination the leisurely pace of other ages.

'Can you see anything?' I heard Jeannie whisper behind me.

I dared not speak. I made a gesture with my hand which meant: 'Yes, I can . . . come and join us.'

It was a young badger just below in the rockery, and oblivious to our gaze he was pushing his black and white striped head into the plants, picking off the clinging snails, and eating them as if he were a small boy eating boiled sweets. He was having a feast; crunch, crunch, crunch . . . there were scores of snails awaiting him, and I watched him move from the waterbutt on my right through a cluster of rudbeckia into a cluster of pansies, then between two of Jeannie's long-legged geraniums into a clump of nicotiana. Perhaps he was the same badger who ate the carrots; the carrots scheduled for Penny and Fred during the winter. He was just as greedy. He did not miss a snail . . . and Oliver and Ambrose, Jeannie and I were fascinated. And the badger himself might have been fascinated had he looked up . . . two cats and two humans observing his indulgence.

Such an incident is of small importance. Some will say that it is pointless even to recall it. Such people are the busy ones who are so active talking about how to improve the world we live in that they have no time for the detail which can make living enjoyable. They proclaim grandiose ideas at Conferences, discuss problems as if they can be solved by computers, and avoid advocating the basic solutions because these can only be reached by the effort of each individual; and individualism is out of fashion.

Thus the busy ones carry on with their Reports, their Campaigns, and their Solutions of all our problems in a haze of generalities which disregard the basic truths. One of the basic truths awaits anyone who has the ears and eyes and sense to recognise it. It requires no law, no Report, no Campaign, no ranting speech read at the Conference rostrum. It lies in gaining pleasure from small, unimportant matters which are everywhere around us waiting to enrich our lives . . . like watching, in the company of Oliver and Ambrose, the activities of a young badger gobbling snails in the moonlight.

I do not, however, consider chasing a mouse in the early hours of the morning a means of gaining pleasure; and this is a task that we have to endure from time to time. They are not mice which come voluntarily into the bedroom. They are the victims of a pounce by Ambrose in some corner of the land outside and are brought in by him in a misguided mood of generosity. Cats everywhere, of course, often have the misconception that a mouse is a welcome present. It is brought into the house with a glad cry and, if dead, deposited on the carpet where it can easily be seen; and when it is removed, thrown with distressing disgust by the recipient into a far section of undergrowth, the donor stalks around in puzzlement. Where has it gone? Why has my present disappeared?

Ambrose, on the other hand, was in favour of live presents. I would be woken up from a sleep by a tally-ho call as he came in through the open window, followed by a thump when he jumped down to the floor. It was a distinctive thump. If he came in minus a present, he jumped to the floor so silently that one might not suspect he had come in . . . but, if he had a present, he chose to behave like a clumsy heavyweight. Thus, when I heard the thump, I would become nervously on guard.

'Do you hear anything?' I murmured on one such occasion, and I had no answer because Jeannie was still asleep, so I lay there and listened.

A rustle to my right in the direction of Jeannie's little walnut desk, and I remembered she had left on the floor a Harrod's box in which was tissue paper.

'Jeannie,' I said again, nudging her. 'Wake up. There's a mouse in the room.'

A convulsion.

'What? What did you say? I'm asleep. I don't want to wake up.'

'It's a mouse. There's a mouse on the floor just beside you . . . can't you hear it?'

Silence for a second, then the rustle again.

'I was having such a lovely sleep.'

We lay still for a while. Perhaps I had been wrong. Perhaps it was just a fluttering moth. This is the customary optimism when you hear the scratch of a mouse. You cannot bear the prospect of dealing with it, so you pretend you have made a mistake . . . and then the noise of it starts up again. The moment of decision has arrived. You either spend the rest of the night half awake, or you go on the attack immediately. We decided to attack.

'Switch on the light and fetch the torch,' said Jeannie. She was always in charge on these occasions. She was a mouse-catching expert. She hated the task, but she followed a method which, although it often took time to be successful, was infallible. The primary aim of this method was to remove the mouse *alive* from the bedroom and deposit it outside into the garden.

The method, needless to say, did not require the aid of Oliver and Ambrose. Cats, in any case, are reluctant to help in such a situation. Mouse catching, in their view, is an outdoor activity or, at any rate, this was the attitude adopted by Monty and Lama in the past, and Oliver and Ambrose in the present. Face them with a mouse on the carpet and they turned away. Push them under a chest of drawers where the mouse was hiding, and they wriggled free and ran. Indoor mouse catching was apparently unfair. The job had better be left to Jeannie.

I shone the torch into a corner.

'There it is! . . . Quick!'

The mouse darted under the bed.

'Damn!'

Jeannie was holding her own particular trap. A cloth. Her object was to manoeuvre the mouse into a position where she could throw the cloth over it, then bravely pick it up, and drop it out of the window.

I heaved the bed to one side, and the mouse disappeared under the William and Mary chest of drawers. I flushed it out from there with a feather duster, and back it scampered under the bed. I was becoming impatient. Another heave of the bed, and away it ran to the Harrod's box.

'I've got it,' cried Jeannie. 'No, I haven't.'

A slippery mouse, it kept us floundering around the small bedroom for twenty minutes or more, making us more and more angry with Ambrose for being the cause of it all. Then, at last, the cry of triumph. Jeannie had caught it and was leaning out of the window, dropping cloth and mouse gently into the nicotiana.

Lights out. Peace again. Then another sound.

Oliver and Ambrose were purring. The chase over, they had come back to bed.

Oliver himself was also the victim of Ambrose's thump. One night Oliver was lying curled up close to me in bed when Ambrose woke me up with a menacing heavyweight thump as he landed on the floor from the window. He stayed a few minutes indoors, then I saw the silhouette of his figure at the window, and he jumped out again, leaving me uncomfortably suspicious that he had left a present behind. However, hearing no scratching noise to disturb me, I soon dozed off.

A while later I was awake again. I had been startled from dreaming by a painful sensation on my face, as if barbed wire had been pulled across it; and it took me only a second to realise that Oliver had dashed over me. No harm, as it turned out, had been done, but it was obvious to me that Oliver had acted in panic. Something had frightened him out of his wits. I switched on the light and, there to my dismay, just at the spot where Oliver had lain curled in slumber was a tiny mouse, the tiniest mouse I had ever seen. No wonder Oliver acted in panic.

We also acted in panic. Jeannie cried out in horror, and I pulled the blanket so violently that the mouse flew to the floor. It was not, however, a mouse. It was, as I learnt later when I looked it up in *Thorburn's Mammals*, a shrew, the lesser or Pigmy shrew to be exact; and Thorburn wrote that 'though hardy as regards severe cold under natural

173

conditions, the constitution of this little animal is extremely frail and sensitive to any kind of shock or untoward circumstances.' Its length from snout to tail was barely two inches.

Naturally, after reading this account, we looked back on the episode with disquiet. If Oliver had been scared into a panic, what about the shrew? It was certainly an untoward circumstance to find itself terrorising a cat, and it was certainly a shock to be chased by Jeannie and myself. Once again, however, Jeannie had shown her skill. True, the chase was prolonged because to catch a two-inch object travelling at speed is bound to be a difficult task . . . but Jeannie, in due course, achieved it. And the Pigmy shrew was carefully deposited out of the window into the garden.

As for Oliver, he had lost his nerve. Not for a fortnight did he return to sleep on the bed.

Oliver was an endearing cat. He endeared himself to us, of course, by the manner he had come into our lives, his patiently conducted conquest of us, the way that Sunday morning he suddenly produced Ambrose as I stood at Monty's Leap. His beginning with us at Minack had become a kind of folk story in our minds, unbelievable unless we had seen it to be real, and a story to hold on to. The impossible *does* occur. Miracles, using the jargon, *do* happen. No need ever to give up hope.

Oliver had a habit which I sometimes found was very touching. I would be sitting or standing at some spot not far from the cottage and enduring a mood of sadness, or inadequacy, or regret, any of those disquieting emotions which inevitably upset one from time to time . . . and Oliver would always appear. He would come up to me and roll upside down, or put his paw on my feet showing that he wanted to jump up, or he would just sit looking at me, yapping. He had become a very talkative cat, and the language varied from tenor-like growls to a sound like someone tuning up on a mouth organ, to the yap. Jeannie was rude about this yap, and the coarse vowel noises which followed. She said that he should take elocution lessons on how to speak.

Oliver had, however, this sense when I needed him, or when Jeannie needed him, an ESP which has never failed us. This black cat which infiltrated into our lives against our wishes was sure that he had a special role to play.

Every few weeks, his namesake would come to see us: Mike Oliver, wartime colonel in the Royal Garhwall Rifles, one of the famous regiments of the British Raj, and who now was in charge of the St Francis Cat and Dog Home at Porth on the outskirts of Newquay. This old friend was a weaver of tweed when we first knew him, living at Mitchell on the noisy A30, alone with a Siamese cat called Ny Ling. He wove beautiful tweed, and many of our friends bought it from him, as we did ourselves . . . but, as a past regular officer of the Royal Garhwall Rifles, he did not possess the ruthless panache of a salesman and, although the tweed was beautiful, the sales were not.

He married a pretty girl called Ruby, who came from Mitchell. As tweed sales fell, he became a life insurance agent and persuasively sold policies to both Jeannie and me; and then, around this time, he was offered the Wardenship of the St Francis Home, which provided him with a bungalow overlooking the Trevelgue Valley at Porth, dog kennels and cattery on the premises, and away from the roar of the A30. They now had a family of two girls and a boy and they decided to accept the offer. Ny Ling went too.

The money for the Home comes from a Trust created by an old Newquay lady in her Will. It is a modest Trust, providing no salary for the Warden other than the benefit of a free home and so, like other such animal homes, the upkeep is largely dependent on charity contributions and the fees obtained for the boarding of cats and dogs when their owners were away.

But such charity contributions and fees never balance the cost of maintaining the stray cats and dogs which come

175

to the Home; and since Mike Oliver never turns a stray away, goes to great trouble and expense to find a home for each one, looks after and feeds them sometimes for months on end before a suitable home is found, it is inevitable that he has to pay out from his own pocket. It is the penalty for being soft-hearted, for having a natural love for animals.

He is, however, a disciplinarian.

'Cats!'

He calls them at meal times as if he were summoning the battalion to the parade ground.

'Cats!'

Ny Ling has gone, and there are thirty cats in his place; cats for whom a home could not be found; cats who, in any case, do not want to leave; straight-haired cats, fluffy cats, tabby cats, elegant cats.

'Cats!'

They come hurrying up the valley field where Dougal and Tufty, the donkeys, are munching grass, out of the armchairs in the bungalow, from various corners around the outhouses. They must not be late. The colonel does not like them to be late.

'Cats!'

They arrive at the assembly point, line up at thirty saucers, and are counted. One is missing.

'Tito! Where's Tito?'

A scurry, and Tito appears. Everything is in order. Dinner begins.

All the family share in the work; Louise, Caroline, John and, of course, Ruby. She is undismayed by animal crises, discovery of kittens left by someone at the door in a box, howling of a dog deserted by a holidaymaker, heartbreak sight of a puppy rescued from drowning after being thrown into the sea by the owner who did not want it . . . she takes such things in her stride and gets on with the practical aspect of looking after the inhabitants of the Home. Others, like the Olivers, in many parts of the country, care for such Homes in the same way. On my own doorstep there is the

Mousehole Bird Hospital founded by the famous Yglesias sisters and which, after being abandoned by the RSPCA, is now struggling for survival, through the efforts of a local committee. In all these Homes, those engaged in running them are doing so for the reward of personal achievement rather than one of money, as in voluntary organisations of any kind. They are the givers. They do not count the hours they work, or belly-ache about their rights. They have a job to do, and set out to do it well.

Caroline Oliver is our god-daughter. She is a slight, fey girl, a Barrie child, and she has a serene confidence in the company of animals which makes her fearless. She is a donkey jockey in the weekly summer races at Newquay, calms temperamental dogs which come to the Home, breaks up a fight however savage, is accepted by any strange cat, and is always acquiring new pets. She arrived one day at Minack in the back of her father's car, a dog sitting in the front seat, nursing a wild baby rabbit and a tiny kitten both sitting on her lap; and quite unself-consciously she carried the kitten into the cottage, sat down on a chair, and proceeded to feed the kitten with milk from an old fashioned fountain pen filler. Then she returned the kitten to the car, where it proceeded to cuddle up with the rabbit.

The dog, a black and white mongrel, meanwhile remained in the car.

'He's a bit odd,' explained Mike. 'It's a pity, but there you are. I've only had him a week.'

'What's wrong?'

'He runs round in circles, brain damage perhaps. It was found running loose on Goss Moor and somebody told the police. Hit by a car no doubt.' Then he added: 'I'll get him better, you'll see.'

The police always notify him when they have an abandoned dog. They rely on him for his help.

'You can take him for a walk,' I said.

Oliver and Ambrose were lying curled on a patch of hay

I had put in the greenhouse specially for them. They were safe because I knew that Mike would put the dog on a lead until he was away from the cottage. He always did so when he brought a dog. A few people, however, advance up the lane with their dog running at random, only to reply, when I gently suggest they control them, that the dog doesn't chase cats or that, if they do, they won't hurt them. I am sure they speak the truth, but I prefer to play safe. Thus I quickly find that the dog is put on the lead when I warn: 'Watch out for Fred! . . . If a dog comes close to him he might kick it over the hedge!'

The dog who went in circles had his walk. He set off in excitement, and returned wishing, no doubt, the walk could have gone on for ever. Once away on his walk he had run hither and thither quite naturally and then, as soon as he returned, he began running in circles again.

The colonel was disappointed, but he had an answer to this setback. A sharp order would bring the dog to his senses. Discipline was a necessity if full capabilities, animal or human, were to be obtained. Flabby attitudes gained nothing. Only encouraged the weak to become weaker.

'Dog!' he commanded. 'Get in the car!'

And the dog immediately jumped in.

A month later I saw Mike again. The dog no longer ran round in circles. He had cured it.

THE LESSER or PIGMY SHREW

TWELVE

The sun on the lintel was returning to the point where it first shone at the beginning of summer. Each evening it moved another inch across the rough surface of the granite, inch by inch until at last it vanished. The sun was no longer setting above the donkey field. Autumn had come.

'I'm still waiting.'

'Waiting for what?' I asked.

Jeannie was pottering in the kitchen, and I was sitting on the sofa, staring up at the lintel.

'You know perfectly well,' she said, coming out of the kitchen, smiling, holding a saucepan in her hand.

I thought, as I looked at her, how lucky I was to have married a girl who was as slim and pretty and feminine as when I first met her, as when the great Cochran had asked her to become one of his Young Ladies and she had refused because she thought it more fun to be Press Officer at the Savoy. Since then, since that moment when she sensed that a life dependent upon mixing with the famous and the ambitious could be over-prolonged, becoming a frivolous vacuum, she had been a peasant, working with her hands in the soil, coping with the primitive life, and never questioning the wisdom of the change. She had learnt the true values; and so she was unaffected by the fact that her book *Meet Me At The Savoy* turned her into a legend, and that her novels *Hotel Regina* and *Home Is The Hotel* had been mentioned in the same category as Arnold Bennett's *Imperial Palace* and Vicki Baum's *Grand Hotel*; and that her paintings and drawings of Minack had been sold all over the world. Her femininity and child-like impetuosity remained, and her contentment.

'Have patience,' I said.

'I've had patience all the year,' she said gently. 'Ever since New Year's Day.'

'Have a little more patience.'

'Doubt in your voice.'

'No, there isn't any doubt . . . I've been thinking about the menu for a long time.'

'A very long time.'

'You could put me off altogether if you make a joke of it.'

'Perhaps that's what you want me to do,' she said, laughing.

'I've even decided upon the first course.'

'What's it to be?'

'Cold cucumber soup.'

She looked at me in astonishment.

'But *I* made the cucumber soup,' she said, 'and it's in the freezer!'

'Ah,' I replied. '*I* grew the cucumbers, and *I* found the recipe.'

'I don't know,' she said, returning to the galley of the kitchen. 'I just don't dare think what the rest of the menu will be like.'

'Nor do I. I'm still thinking it up.'

'Don't strain yourself.'

I continued to sit in my corner of the sofa, staring up at the lintel.

I was thinking of the other inhabitants of Minack who had watched the sun come and go on the lintel. Mystery people who had spent their lives here, leaving no record of their time except the old stone hedges in the fields around us, the carved out meadows on the cliffs, the ancient barn with its granite slabs bound together by clay, the little well beside the lane, the trees they had planted for shelter, the great rocks they had touched, and the cottage with its solid chimney and its arm length thick walls, the dome of the bread oven perfectly built with its small stones, and the lintel above the fireplace where burning furze kept them warm when the gales blew.

Perhaps it was sparks from one furze which set the thatched roof alight many years ago. It was a fire, one would have thought, that would have stayed in the minds of those who lived in St Buryan parish; a story that would have been handed on by parents to their children. Yet, until recently, I never could discover what had happened. Old men of the village, always ready to tell a story, could tell me nothing of the details, only contradictory dates of when it happened . . . 1916 said one, 1922 said another. 'Another world down Minack,' I would be told. 'I've lived in the village all my life and never been down Minack.' They pronounce Minack as Mynack, and it is the local shortened version of Dorminack, the formal name for the cottage. It has always been thus. No one in the parish ever calls the cottage by any name but Minack.

This summer, however, I discovered the truth about the fire at the cottage, but there is still a question mark as to how it started. I had a visit from an elderly lady who had been away from the area for many years, and she had come on a pilgrimage to see the playground of her youth. She had been brought up in one of the three cottages which face the sea a mile or so westwards along the coast, hidden from us by a hill, and where Jane Wyllie of *A Drake at the Door* used to live.

She told me that as a child she used to play games with her friends around Minack and she pointed to a great slab of a rock which juts out from the cottage and said they used to dance barefoot upon it; and years, years later it was the same rock that A. P. Herbert used to romance upon, saying that he was sure it was a rock of magic.

Then she went on to tell us that in 1912 the cottage was empty except that it was used as a store for furniture belonging to the Trewern family who, at that time, farmed Rosemodress, the farm at the top of the hill. Old man Trewern, who was blind, I had often been told about, and he had caught my imagination. He used to come down the curving lane from Rosemodress guided by his stick and, when he reached Minack, crossing Monty's Leap, then up the lane towards the cottage, he stopped when he reached the barn where the old horse of the farm was stabled. He would then go into the stable, and sit down on a stool which was kept there, and listen. Listen to the shifting of the old horse's hooves, listen to him munching the hay in a trough, listen in his mind to the days when the horse led the plough around Minack.

It was in 1912, apparently, that the cottage caught fire and the thatched roof and all the contents were gutted. Obviously there had been no fire-fighting equipment available, mechanised or horse drawn, and so there was no hope for the cottage. Yet it did not char into oblivion. One might even say that, except for the thatched roof, little damage was done. The walls were too thick to be affected, and the lintel too massive.

Massive enough to be there fifty, a hundred, two hundred years into the future; and I wonder whose eyes and what kind of people will be looking at it then.

I have ideas as to what kind of people I would like them to be. I would like people to live here who do not adopt a façade, acting as if effect is of greater value than reality. I would like them to believe that life is a mystery and not an organisation ruled by human beings. I would not like them to be people who are envious of others, who spend more time looking for faults than appreciating virtues; and I would not like them to be social butterflies who prefer chatter to silence. I would like them to be aware of the past, relish the present, and be not too concerned about the future. I would not like them to have orderly minds, because orderly minds would object to the inconvenience of living far from the routine of a housing centre. I would like them to be dreamers, irrational people who are not enslaved by conventional attitudes and contemporary fads; and, as a result, they would be so immersed in the magic of Minack that they would find themselves believing that they had lived here before. They would be stayers, therefore. They would not run away when winter came. They would belong.

Our predecessors, however, never had reason to romance in this way. They lived in the age of innocence. They believed in King and Country, in God, and weather signs in the sky. They were free to be themselves, came slowly to conclusions without being brainwashed by television pundits, or hemmed in by a multitude of laws they did not understand, or by ever-increasing taxes which forced them to give up their pleasures. Life may have been hard for them in many ways, but at least it was simple.

It was simple, for instance, for Harry Ladner. Harry Ladner, who had died some years previously, was the last long-time resident of the cottage before our arrival. Captain Harry he was called; a courtesy title, a title of fun, for he had never been a captain of any sort. He was, too, a man of fun and in between scratching a livelihood from catching rabbits, growing early potatoes, having a few pigs, a cow or two, and daffodils, he would spend much time at the Wink, the pub at Lamorna. There he would regale the customers, those who were strangers, with unlikely stories of the Cornish countryside so colourfully that his glass was never empty. His was an art, a dying art, of entertaining visitors, holding them enthralled with splendid local stories of wreckers and highwaymen and ghosts and stirring stories of the sea. The visitors were delighted, the locals smiled; and when time was called Captain Harry would set out to stagger back to Minack. It was a rough walk, up and down, boulders to trip him up, hedges to climb, and so often, if the weather were fine, he would take a rest amongst the bracken and sleep the night away.

'Ah, Harry Ladner,' I have heard old men say. 'He was a case!'

He was, however, a happy man. He was also, in his own small way, an impresario. He had good timing. He sensed when the occasion was correct to tell this story or that; and he only brought forth his special blockbuster at rare intervals and, only then, if he were sure that no one present had been present at any previous occasion. Had I heard him tell it, I do not think I would have believed him, but I am told that so convincing was he, such a natural con man in fact, that I would have joined every other listener in breathlessly awaiting the outcome of this particular blockbuster.

He would ask his listeners whether they had ever known five rabbits being shot with one bullet from a rifle; and, of course, they would reply that such a deed was impossible. Thereupon he would hold up a bullet in his hand and tell his audience that, if they came back the following evening, he would show them five rabbits all shot by the one bullet. Couldn't he easily cheat? Oh no, he had never cheated, and he promised faithfully that only the one bullet would be fired. His glass was filled again and again, and then he staggered back to Minack.

Next evening at the Wink the customers waited. Seven o'clock, eight o'clock, no sign of Captain Harry . . . and then triumphantly he arrived, carrying five shot rabbits attached to a stick.

'There you are,' he said. 'All five shot by a single bullet.'

'How can you prove it?'

'Ah,' he snorted and, in my mind, I imagine that he was talking like Chris Gittins as the immortal Walter Gabriel of *The Archers*, 'I don't have to prove it. They are there. I just waited until the five of them was lined up in a row.'

More glasses, many more glasses were filled, and once more he returned unsteadily to Minack.

The rumbustious charm of such people is disappearing, partly because television is smoothing away the rough edges of those who live in isolated hamlets, and partly because bureaucratic and commercial forces are determined to eliminate the elusive quality of Cornwall. This elusive quality has its roots in a mysticism which is foreign to a materialistic society and is difficult to defend. Why, for instance, should a desolate moorland, home of foxes, badgers, rabbits and wild birds, be treated as sacred when a housing estate on the site would provide hundreds of homes? Why should a caravan on a headland be considered unsightly when the farming community are allowed to erect vast hangers of barns wherever they wish without official consent? Why shouldn't there be chalets close to a beach, providing holidays for factory workers and others? Why shouldn't it be allowed to build a house on the coast?

Logical answers to such questions are a problem to find. Anything to do with subtlety, sensitivity and taste, is difficult to explain to those who are conditioned into believing that economic indexes provide the criterion for happiness; and it is made the more difficult when one realises that in this age of mania of equality the comparative few appreciate beauty. The majority are happy crowded on Blackpool sands or the Costa Brava. The majority like noise, queueing, wearing funny hats, and simple foods like fish and chips. Nothing wrong in that. But it is sad, I feel, when they move out of their established enclaves and proceed to uproot those who do not share their standards; and are encouraged to do so, for gain, both by bureaucratic and commercial forces.

West Cornwall at the present time, for instance, is under siege. The developers and the roadmakers have been creeping down the spine of Cornwall for the past few years, employing their earth-moving machines to gouge away the countryside, building zombie housing estates around ancient villages, and erecting monstrous edifices in old town centres like that of Truro, where the beautiful cathedral is squashed against a multi-storey car park. Nothing that the developers produce can be admired. All is functional . . . the hideous multiple stores, carbon copies of those in Birmingham, Streatham or Derby; the squat, massive insurance and building society offices which sprout like mushrooms in every High Street, and even the hoardings which advertise the housing estates. There is one such hoarding on the top of Paul Hill above Newlyn, which has been there for five years . . . suitable for commuter belt country, but a running sore for those who prefer to forget the existence of developers in the wild land of the far west.

The Road, however, offers the biggest menace. The Road is the brainchild of the Department of the Environment and its offshoot, the Western Road Construction Unit. The Unit has been responsible for the motorways of the West Country and, despite there being several really necessary routes to develop, such as from Truro to Falmouth and from Falmouth to Helston, it has fixed its attention upon creating the Road to Penzance.

One stretch requiring two hundred acres of farmland will run from Camborne to St Erth where the present A30 turns off to St Ives; and the second stretch will run from St Erth to the Heliport at the entrance of Penzance, requiring another one hundred acres of farmland. One suspects that the main purpose of the Road is to provide jobs for the Unit and the contractors involved . . . for no one in the area has any wish for it.

After all, the Road can only lead to Land's End and the sea . . . and, except in the short period of peak August holiday traffic, the present road is a motorist's paradise, so sparse is the traffic. Hence millions of taxpayers' money is about to be wasted, at the same time as bringing to a stop the kind of tourist who is so vital to the economy of West Cornwall.

But if there are those outside Cornwall who are determined to destroy the beauty of Cornwall, there are many people within the county who are equally determined to stop them. These are not just Canute-minded members of Conservation Groups . . . they are local councillors, county councillors and members of the public, who are becoming ever increasingly aware that the mystical charm of Cornwall could vanish in a decade if the developers have their way. The control of caravan sites, for instance, is an example of what has been achieved.

The long-established caravan sites, those that sprawl like fungi on various coastal stretches, will, unfortunately, have to remain . . . but any new caravan site, even if it is permitted, is subject to very stringent planning control. Often this means that the site has a dual purpose, being a home for touring caravans in the summer, but reverting to grazing pasture for cattle during the rest of the year. Hence there is no permanent disfigurement of the landscape. I am thinking, at this moment, of two recently established caravan sites, that of Treverven a few miles from Minack, and of Trelowarren, ancient home of the Vyvyan family near the Helford River. Neither of these gives offence; and there are other smaller ones, attached to farms, like the one at Boleigh which we pass on the way to Penzance, that are inconspicuous.

Thus, although once I was a critic of the caravan holiday, I am now in favour. The only snag about such a holiday affects the holidaymakers themselves. They swop household chores for caravan chores, and the Jeannies of this world have to continue with their cooking.

That sentence reminds me of my own self-indulgent behaviour. I have taken Jeannie's efforts in the kitchen too long for granted. I sit ruminating on the sofa while she is fussing over pots and pans and preparing delicacies to delight me. It is time I fulfilled the last of my New Year resolutions. I must cook a meal she will remember.

I wish I could say that the meal was a complete success. It was nearly so, but I made a stupid mistake at the end. The menu I chose was as follows:–

Cucumber Soup
Sole Miroton with Pommes de Terre Duchesse.
Cape Gooseberry Flan.

The cucumber soup, I have already admitted, came from the freezer. The choice of *Sole Miroton* was a matter of luck. I took from the bookshelf a copy of Madame Prunier's Fish Cookery Book, the same copy that inspired me years before at Mortlake, opened a page at random, shut my eyes, and dabbed my finger on the recipe for *Sole Miroton*. It read:

Poach the fillets flat with white wine and fish fumet. Dish them on a rather creamy mushroom purée, and scatter on the fillets some roughly chopped *fines herbes* (Parsley, chervil, chives and tarragon).
Cover with highly seasoned Bercy Sauce, and brown quickly.

The Cape Gooseberry flan I chose because I had grown a number of Cape Gooseberry plants from seed and each plant had grown into a mammoth size in the greenhouse and had a proliferation of fruit. We had not expected such a proliferation. We had grown them because Jeannie has a particular liking for the Cape Gooseberry coated in sugar which is served with Friandises in restaurants. We did not, however, realise until we grew them, that they were also a winter fruit, a delicious, sweet gooseberry which needed no cooking and was ideal for tarts and flans.

Thus the menu was set, a Sunday lunchtime was chosen as the occasion, and the necessary materials obtained. Soon after breakfast on the appointed day, I persuaded Jeannie to disappear from the cottage for the morning; and she went away in a state of apprehension. She could not believe that my *Sole Miroton* could be anything but a disaster.

I too, as I stood alone in the kitchen, was in a state of apprehension. My high-sounding promises had reached the moment of action. I had to prepare a fish fumet, and a fish velouté for the Bercy Sauce.

Put four tablespoonfuls of white wine and the same of fish fumet in a saucepan [read the recipe for Bercy Sauce] with a dessertspoonful of chopped shallot, and reduce it by a third. Add not quite half a pint of fish velouté, bring to the boil, and finish with two ounces of butter and a teaspoonful of chopped parsley.

Keep calm, I said to myself, read the instructions carefully, don't hurry, and above all don't lose your nerve. Your character is being put to the test.

At that moment there was a miaow at my feet.

'Oliver!'

There was another miaow, a squeak of a miaow.

'Ambrose!'

I greeted them as one greets old friends in a moment of crisis. The rush of warmth, the sudden easing of tension. It did not matter to me that they had ulterior motives. I just felt grateful for their presence.

Thus, as I cooked, they watched my progress . . . the stewing of the fish bones, the sieving through a strainer, the making of a *roux* (flour and butter), the simmering, the preparation of the mushroom purée and the potatoes and, finally, after Jeannie had returned, the poaching of the sole.

'And now,' I said, when I had finished. 'You can be the official tasters.'

And they gobbled a fillet.

Jeannie did not gobble. She slowly savoured my delicacy. She even declared it a triumph of *haute cuisine*. She declared that *Sole Miroton* was one of the great fish dishes of the world . . . and such was her praise that I doffed my imaginary chef's hat again and again after our plates were empty.

Then came the Cape Gooseberry flan.

And this *was* a disaster.

I set it down confidently on the table, produced a bowl of Cornish cream, and cut two slices. They were uneatable.

In cooking the pastry I had made a fundamental mistake. I had mixed the pastry and fashioned it into the circular tin, then failed to pre-heat the oven. Thus my flan went into a cold oven; and the consequence was pastry with the consistency of cardboard.

Jeannie's only comment was to suggest that the gulls on the roof would enjoy it; and the donkeys if there were still some to spare; and Broadbent.